Darlington Raceway

50th Anniversary

ACKNOWLEDGMENTS

UMI Publications, Inc., is pleased to present the Darlington Raceway 50th Anniversary book, commemorating 50 years of racing at NASCAR's original superspeedway and the historic Southern 500.

Darlington Raceway's tale is filled with colorful, genuinely interesting stories, from how founder Harold Brasington acquired the land to construct the track (a verbal agreement during a poker game in a tobacco warehouse in 1948), to its present-day status as one of the most revered and difficult tracks on the NASCAR Winston Cup Series circuit.

We invite you to join us as author Jim Hunter chronicles in loving detail the history of a facility once known as The Lady in Black. As president of Darlington Raceway, no one knows her better than Hunter. As a boy, he listened to Darlington's spectacular events on the radio, and later served as its public relations director in the late 1960s. His early ties with the track launched an award-winning motorsports journalism career – a springboard to a series of high-ranking positions within NASCAR, which brought him back to Darlington, this time as its president. The Track Too Tough To Tame is in his heart, as well as his blood. We would particularly like to thank Mr. Hunter for his hard work and dedication to bringing the history of the great track to life on the pages of this book for all to enjoy.

In addition to Mr. Hunter, we would like to thank the staff at Darlington Raceway for their invaluable assistance and contributions in preparing this book, including opening their vast photo archives to provide to you, a pictorial history of this venerable facility. To Herbert Ames, Bridget Blackwell, Jenny Griffin, Mac Josey, Harold King, Clarice Lane, Norma Nesbitt, Karen Rose, and Sammie Yarborough, we thank you.

This book also would not be possible without the help and guidance of our friends at NASCAR. We would like to express our thanks and appreciation to Mr. Bill France, Mr. Jim France, Mr. Mike Helton, Mr. Brian France, Mr. George Pyne, Mr. John Griffin, Ms. Kelly Crouch and Mr. Paul Schaefer.

Most of all, we thank you, the fans of NASCAR racing in general, and of Darlington Raceway in particular. It is you who have made this sport possible, and who are responsible for its continued growth and success. This commemorative publication is for you, with our gratitude. We sincerely hope you will enjoy this book.

UMI Publications, Inc. Staff: *President and Publisher* – Ivan Mothershead; *Vice President and Associate Publisher* – Charlie Keiger; *Vice President* – Rick Peters; *Controller* – Lewis Patton; *National Advertising Manager* – Mark Cantey; *Advertising Account Executive* – Paul Kaperonis; *Managing Editor* – Ward Woodbury; *Associate Editor* – John Bisci; *Art Director* – Brett Shippy; *Senior Designers* – Mike McBride and Paul Bond; *Manager of Information Systems* – Chris Devera; *Customer Service Representatives* – Mary Flowe, Carla Greene, Heather Guy, Joanie Tarbert

---

This book is officially licensed by Darlington Raceway and NASCAR.

ISBN 0-943860-15-6

FOREWORD

by Cathy Best Mock – Editor of Darlington News & Press and Five O'clock Friday

Darlington Raceway is quiet today.

The historic track is calm and peaceful in these early morning hours. The air is still and humid and heavy with the sweet smell of honeysuckle; the famous black "stripes" where drivers with last names like Earnhardt, Jarrett and Petty have made contact with the concrete retaining wall appear no more threatening than a child's muddy handprints on a white kitchen wall.

"You don't look so tough to me," a casual observer might be tempted to whisper.

Don't let Jim Hunter hear you say that. She may look deserted, but Darlington Raceway is not alone this morning. It's 7:45 a.m., and the Raceway is waking up. Hunter is her alarm clock.

Jim Hunter, president of Darlington Raceway and an advocate for the sport of NASCAR auto racing long before it was considered socially acceptable, is simultaneously talking with a contractor on his cell phone about the nearly-completed new grandstand in turn four, planning a press conference to honor Darlington's legendary drivers, and steering his way through the infield to check on preparations for a promotional event in the NASCAR Winston Cup garage scheduled for later in the day.

"This place is special; she's always been special, and she always will be," says Hunter, who, since coming to Darlington as president of the Raceway in 1993, has weathered criticism and comments calling the fabled oval everything from a dinosaur to a dump.

Seven years later, Darlington Raceway looks anything but prehistoric. Her new grandstands glint and gleam in the early morning sun; state-of-the-art media and medical facilities sit in a beautifully landscaped infield. Rows of graceful palmettos, South Carolina's state tree, line the corporate hospitality village.

Famous old sayings about sleeping dragons and still waters could also be reasonably applied to NASCAR's original superspeedway 50 weeks out of the year. She appears tame and relatively harmless, but as race weekend approaches she takes on the aspect of a woman getting ready for a party.

Her apparel combines the bright shades of M&Ms candies and a DuPont rainbow; she becomes Budweiser's "Lady in Red" and cinches the safety belt on Goodwrench's little black dress. The perfume she dabs behind her ears and on her wrists smells like gas, oil and exhaust fumes. She is the most beautiful woman in all the world, and she will hypnotize you and make you court her and fall in love with her.

And, if you don't – she'll chew you up and spit you back out. She is, indeed, a tough old broad.

North Charleston, South Carolina, native Jim Hunter always loved sports, and describes himself as "the typical high school jock. Football, baseball, track; you name it, I played it," he says.

As a child, Hunter listened to the Southern 500 on the radio, drinking in what he calls "the power and the sounds," rooting for guys with intriguing names like Fireball Roberts, Banjo Matthews and Cotton Owens; now, he was experiencing it up close and personal for the first time.

"I was hooked," he says.

Throughout his career, Hunter has supported and promoted NASCAR, literally, from the tires up – he once worked for Firestone, for Chrysler, and as a writer, public relations director and fan of the sport.

He attributes much of his success to the example set not only by the entire France family, but also by the entire NASCAR family. "There are no finer Americans in the country or the world than those associated with this sport," he says. "They believe in God, country, and earning what you get through hard work. And, I'll tell you something; there are plenty of people who are smarter than me, brighter than me – but they can't outwork me."

Although he worked and traveled all over the country in the course of his career, Hunter says he always maintained his ties to the Darlington Raceway and the friends he had made in the Darlington community. When he was sent to the Raceway as president in 1993, it was like a homecoming for him.

Darlington Raceway ushered in stock car racing's new era in 1950 with a unique design and a layer of asphalt, and she has carried the standard for every NASCAR Winston Cup track constructed since, large or small. It hasn't always been an easy fight, but time after time she has emerged victorious, with her standard held high for the entire sports world to see.

And just as Darlington Raceway has borne – and set – the standard for the sport of NASCAR, so Jim Hunter has carried the standard for Darlington Raceway.

"If I died tomorrow, I would die knowing there is a place for Darlington in the future of this sport."

CONTENTS

INTRODUCTION

Darlington President Jim Hunter and driver Jeremy Mayfield proudly unveil the "50th Anniversary Southern 500 at Darlington" logo.

It wasn't all that long ago when a typical stock car racing social encounter went something like this.

People would ask, "By the way, what line of work are you in?"

By the time you finished your response, "I'm in the stock car racing business," the person asking had given you one of those, "Heaven forbid, forgive-me-for-asking looks" and abruptly shifted his or her attention in a new direction.

"Well," you'd think, "Excuse me!" and sort of add as an afterthought to yourself, "Excuse me for being alive!"

The reason I bring this up in an introduction to a book on the historic occasion of Darlington Raceway's 50th Pepsi Southern 500 celebration is this: NASCAR and stock car racing aren't that long ago removed from its image of being from the "other side of the tracks." The wrong side. Stock car racing used to be politically incorrect and socially unacceptable.

Richard Petty – our sport's No. 1 spokesperson of all time – put things in perspective for the everyday American many years ago, and "The King's" words still ring true today.

"One of the things all us boys have to remember is our raisin'. We were

A ticket for the very first Southern 500. At a mere $5.00, they sold out fast, so those without tickets simply knocked the fences down.

brought up to respect our elders. We say 'yes sir' and 'yes ma'am' to folks older than us. We're brought up to love our families and to love our country. We salute our flag. We stand at attention when the Star Spangled Banner is played. We go to church on Sunday, when we can. And, last but not least, we work hard for everything we get."

NASCAR racing might have changed over the years, but its roots are still the same. God. Country. Family. And no free rides. Whatever you get, you earn.

Darlington Raceway has earned its place in NASCAR history. For one thing, it was first. The very first. There were no other asphalt tracks conducting 500-mile races for stock cars when Darlington was built. How it was built is a story in itself – a great story – and you'll enjoy reading it in this book.

During the 1960s and '70s, NASCAR racing was considered a common man's sport – blue-collar entertainment. But over the years, I've known more lawyers, judges, doctors, accountants, developers and politicians who attended NASCAR events than all the blue-collar workers combined. In the past few years it has become acceptable (politically correct) to be a NASCAR fan.

They're calling it a "phenomenon."

I call it common sense. The masses are discovering what people in the South have known for years: Stock car racing is exciting! It's fun! It's "in!"

This book carries you from Darlington's unbelievable beginning to her 50th birthday. Along the way, we hope that readers gather insight into NASCAR's evolution as a major league American sport. And without Darlington Raceway, NASCAR might not be where it is today.

And without NASCAR, Darlington Raceway would certainly not be where it is today. The two were a perfect match 50 years ago. Who would have believed it?

I'm from South Carolina, and I'm just as proud of that as anything in the world – except for my family, especially my two grandsons, Dakota James Hunter and Hunter James McKernan. If you have a few minutes sometime, I'll be glad to show you a few thousand pictures taken by their grandmother (appropriately called "Go-Go" by the boys) in the space of just a few years!

When I was growing up, Darlington Raceway was the only track of its kind in South Carolina. In fact, Darlington Raceway was not just the biggest stock car racing track in South Carolina, it was the only paved, strictly-stock car track in the entire United States.

Darlington has been special to me for as long as I

Actors Alan Hale (standing, left) and Rory Calhoun (inside the car) make a pit stop during the filming of "Thunder In Carolina" at Darlington in 1959. Hale later played "The Skipper" on the Gilligan's Island TV show.

can remember. Just as I grew up eating homemade biscuits and redeye gravy, I grew up with Darlington Raceway.

I listened to the Southern 500 on the radio, just like I listened to the old Charleston Rebels of the Sally League. I tried to keep up with the race by writing down the leaders as they were announced by Darlington Raceway's announcing team, Dave "Eye In The Sky" Rodgers and Johnny Evans. It was Rodgers who helped me break into the sport years later by introducing me around when I was covering racing for the Columbia State and Columbia Record newspapers.

It seems like only yesterday when I closed my eyes and listened as Evans described the action. "Fireball Roberts has the lead and rides the rail through Darlington's treacherous third turn. Right on his bumper is Banjo Matthews with Junior Johnson in third!"

Everyone had a nickname back then. Nicknames like Fireball, Banjo, Junior, Cotton or Possum. Herman Beam was known as "The Turtle." He was a nice man – a mechanical engineer with degree from the University of North Carolina – who chose to chase his dreams on the Grand National circuit of NASCAR as a car owner/driver.

Herman didn't want to tear his car up - it was the only one he had - so he didn't run as fast as most of the cars and simply relied on finishing power. ("You got to be there at the end," is the way Bill Elliott put it years later.)

Beam was the classic example of the tortoise and the hare, and members of the press used to place wagers on whether Herman The Turtle would finish higher in the race than such noted chargers as Junior Johnson and Glen (Fireball) Roberts. And more often than not, Herman did indeed finish ahead of them.

There are other nicknames in the colorful history of Darlington Raceway and NASCAR. Banjo's name was Edwin Matthews. Junior's name was Robert Glen Johnson. Fireball was Glen Roberts and his nickname came from his fastball. Cotton was Everette Owens.

There was also DeWayne "Tiny" Lund, a big man with a big heart and a heavy foot who came from Iowa and built a fishing camp on the shores of the Santee-Cooper reservoir not far from Darlington. He never won at Darlington, but stock cars fans loved big ol' Tiny.

There was Elzie Wylie Baker. Folks called him "Buck." Let's just say that Buck had a mean streak folks today

In 1994, Tyler Tower, which overlooks the frontstretch, opened. This photo depicts the tower's beginnings. Supervising the construction are (l to r) track superintendent Sammie Yarborough, current track president Jim Hunter and former president Walter D. "Red" Tyler, for whom the tower is named.

refer to as a "commitment to winning," regardless of the odds. Buck Baker drove to win.

Buck had a son, Elzie Wylie Baker Jr., who also played a large role in the development of the sport. Folks called him "Buddy" for the same reason they called his daddy Buck. Buddy Baker was a force at Darlington and loved the old track like family.

"Darlington was like family," says Buddy, who now does commentary for NASCAR telecasts. "Everybody knew everybody, and everybody knew you had to race the old track as well, or more than, the other cars and drivers. It was a place where a part of you hated the track and a part of you loved it."

One thing has never changed, though: No matter how many races a driver might win in a career, if he hasn't won at Darlington, there's an asterisk next to his name - at least among the drivers, anyway. You haven't made it if you haven't won at Darlington. All the drivers know that. That's why they still want to win there. It's still the toughest, and the most demanding. If a driver wins at Darlington, he can win anywhere.

Here's the real kicker to this introductory few pages of trivia regarding 50 years of Darlington Raceway. The drivers drove their cars to the track to compete in that first Southern 500, 50 years ago. Stock car racing really was "stock car" racing!

The only difference in the cars from the ones you drove on the highways (there were no interstates back then – they weren't a part of our everyday life until President Eisenhower sold Congress on the idea of interstate highways as vital to our country's defense), were some beefed-up parts, taped-up headlights and taillights and fine-tuned engines.

Advertising for the races back then referred to the events as "strictly-stock" stock car races. This was to differentiate these "stock cars" from the Modifieds that typically ran on old fairground dirt tracks throughout the country. These Modifieds had special racing engines and other speed parts designed for dirt-track racing.

Stock car racing's advertising and marketing have really changed. And you'll read examples of the changes throughout the following pages in the context of when things changed and why.

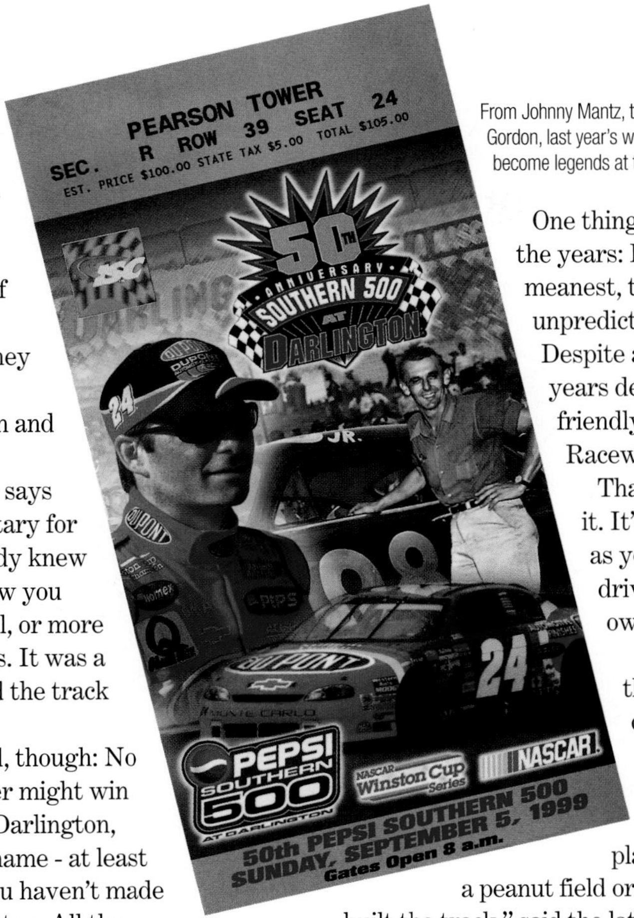

From Johnny Mantz, the winner of the first Southern 500, to Jeff Gordon, last year's winner of the Pepsi Southern 500, drivers have become legends at the landmark facility that is "Too Tough To Tame."

One thing has remained constant over the years: Darlington Raceway is still the meanest, toughest, most unforgiving and unpredictable old track in America. Despite a cosmetic makeover in recent years designed to offer a more fan-friendly atmosphere, Darlington Raceway is still special.

That's what I've always liked about it. It's a special place. You can feel it as you walk through the gates. The drivers feel it. The crews and car owners feel it.

More than once in the pages that follow, you'll read where a driver says something absolutely ugly about this old place.

A few exclamations come to mind. "They ought to plow this place up again and turn it back into a peanut field or whatever it was before they built the track," said the late Bobby Isaac, a Hall of Famer and 1970 NASCAR Winston Cup Series champion.

And NASCAR Busch Series star Randy Lajoie, never at a loss for words, had this to say during his victory celebration interview following a race. "I'll tell you the toughest part of the track here at Darlington. The toughest part is any time you leave pit road and go on the race track. It's the toughest track in NASCAR"

"They ought to fill this place up with water and turn it into a bass fishing pond," Kyle Petty exclaimed after he had hit her unforgiving wall.

Located where it is, Darlington Raceway is just a hop, skip and river rock throw from just about anywhere. Columbia, the capital of the state, is less than 70 miles west. Charlotte, N.C., is less than 100 miles north. Charleston – America's most historic city, in my opinion – is a couple of hours to the southeast, and Myrtle Beach – vacation paradise to hundreds of thousands of golfers and families – is little more than 90 miles to the east on the Atlantic coast.

So, let's get on with the first 50 years of Darlington Raceway. It's the most incredible race track in the world. Read on – you'll understand what I mean.

Jim Hunter
President, Darlington Raceway

The FABULOUS FIFTIES

(Above) Harold Brasington's dream became a reality in 1950. Here, he, along with his son Harold Jr., wife Mildred and Fred Stem, an original member of the track's Board of Directors, stand in front of a billboard on the Raceway grounds.

(Right) The frontstretch begins to take shape in 1950.

Harold Brasington had been thinking about it for quite some time: a paved race track in Brasington's hometown of Darlington, South Carolina. "It was sometime in the 1930s – I don't exactly remember when I first took the notion to build it," Brasington recalled many years later. He had attended America's biggest automobile race, the Indianapolis 500. "That got me to thinking. I thought about it for a lot of years." But Brasington's plans, like everyone's plans in America at the time, took a back seat to World War II.

After the war, Harold was trying to build a sand-and-gravel business to feed his young family, just like other struggling young fathers were doing. In his spare time, Harold kept thinking about his big track in Darlington.

"When I was up there at Indianapolis and saw that crowd of people," said Brasington while reminiscing with a group of writers at Darlington in the early 1990s, "I figured if they could draw 200,000 people to watch Indy cars there, we could get lots of people to watch a different kind of race in the South. I had to put my idea on hold for quite a spell because I was trying to build the trucking business and trying to figure out how to raise the money. Then the war came along, so that sort of put things on the back burner for a spell."

Jean Thurmond, wife of then South Carolina Governor Strom Thurmond, cut the ribbon for the first Southern 500 on September 4, 1950. Looking on is (l to r) NASCAR President Bill France Sr., a NASCAR official, Thurmond and Harold Brasington, who built the landmark facility.

Brasington thought what would appeal to people would be "drivers racing the same cars the farmer, the worker, the doctor and so forth drive back and forth to work every day and to church every Sunday."

Planned or unplanned, Brasington's thoughts coincided philosophically with the ideas floating around in the mind of another widely-known and well-respected pioneer in the auto racing business, William H.G. "Big Bill" France, who was just getting established in Daytona Beach, Florida.

Stock cars – family cars, passenger cars, everyday cars that everyday people drove – were the cars that were beginning to be raced on dirt fairgrounds throughout the Southeast. It was Harold's notion that people would want to see that type of car racing on a big track like Indianapolis, a track he planned to build in Darlington.

Nothing would happen until 1949, well after the War, but Harold was busily doing the legwork to make it happen. He used speaking opportunities at every civic club that would have him, in an effort to raise money for the project.

"Most folks around here thought Harold had lost his mind," said lifelong Darlington resident Harold King, known affectionately as "Mr. Darlington" within social circles in South Carolina for his lifelong civic contributions and longtime involvement as an insider at the Raceway. "Harold Brasington was as committed to building the race track as a man can be committed to something, but he certainly didn't have an easy road getting people to put hard-earned money into his idea. Some folks even thought he might be a little 'tetched in the head,' to borrow one of my grandmamma's old sayings."

Nonetheless, when September rolled around in 1949, Brasington had accumulated enough equipment to start building his track. All he needed was a place to build it.

How the site for Brasington to build his track was chosen is a story in itself, and Anthony Brown was there the night Harold Brasington and J.S. (Sherman) Ramsey made the deal. Brown is a grandson of Darlington's Sherman Ramsey. His mother, Helen Colt Ramsey Brown, was the older sister of J.S. (Jack) Ramsey Jr., Sherman's son.

"I do not know whether the idea for a race track at Darlington was conceived at the poker table that evening of September 4, 1948, or whether it was simply solidified," Brown recalls. "I do know that the deal was done and the bargain stood on the word of two men without so much as a handshake.

"The legal process came later, but only after bulldozers had begun ripping up the east end of my grandfather's (J.S. Ramsey Sr.) country property, the former DuBose Plantation, a 600-acre tract that Grandfather had bought during the years of The Depression. We all called it 'The Farm.'

"After Helen Ramsey Brown, my mother, died in April 1947, and my father, Allen E. Brown, moved to Knoxville, Tennessee, to open a branch of the Darlington Veneer Company called Diamond Hill Plywood Company, I went to live with my mother's parents, the late J.S. and Helen Colt Ramsey, at their home on Spring Street in Darlington.

"It was my grandfather's habit to walk into town after supper, sometimes to play poker with other businessmen, and afterwards, to visit the county jail near the town square. (The County jail and the Darlington Police Department were places where men would commonly gather to talk politics or just shoot the bull.) On some occasions, but only on weekends, he would ask me to go with him.

"His reason for visiting the jail was personal. If any of his workers from the Darlington Veneer Company were in jail for over-drinking or any other reason, he would bail them out so they would be at work by 6 a.m. on Monday.

"At about 7:30 on that September Saturday evening in 1948, my grandfather and I walked to the Center Brick Tobacco Warehouse on South Main Street where he joined Fred Stem, owner of the warehouse and host for the evening, Clyde DeWitt, Judge Ed Dennis, Harold Brasington and another man whose name I do not recall, making a table of six players for poker.

"They sat down at a well-lighted round table near the warehouse entrance while I went off to play on some empty

A glorious sight – the starting lineup for NASCAR's original superspeedway race, the Southern 500 at Darlington.

The pace car leads the field into turn one prior to the historic start of the first Southern 500 at Darlington on Sept. 4, 1950.

tobacco skids. I was told that if I approached the table, to stand behind my grandfather – I supposed, so I could not see the other players' hands.

"At about 10 p.m., near my bedtime, I came to the table. Standing behind my grandfather, I heard the following conversation between hands in the poker game."

"Mr. Ramsey," asked Mr. Brasington, "what do you plan to do with your land out on the Hartsville road?" This was State Road 151-34. My Grandfather's farm lay four miles from central Darlington at that time.

"There are some tenant farmers at the west end of the property," my grandfather replied. "I use the remainder of the property for bird hunting. There are some old cabins on that part of the property that date back to pre-war days (in reference to the War Between the States of 1860-65) and there's a barn near the dirt road that leads down to my pond and clubhouse."

Almost as an afterthought, my grandfather said, "Why do you ask?"

"Let's build a race track on the east end," Brasington said, "near the Hartsville road."

Preoccupied with the poker game, my grandfather gave Brasington a cursory, "Sure," and then added, "Now deal the cards!"

"We walked home about 10:30 and my grandmother met us at the door, scolding Grandfather for keeping me out so late. But when he reminded her it was Saturday night, she calmed down."

Brown said Labor Day fell on September 6 that year (1948). Approximately one week later, his grandfather went to Knoxville to visit his father, then went on to Norfolk, Virginia, to look into opening another branch of Diamond Hill Plywood.

"Grandfather returned to Darlington by way of U.S. Highway 52 into the north part of town, and my grandmother met him at the door with a question: 'What in the world are you doing out at the farm?'"

"Why, nothing," my grandfather replied.

A total of 75 drivers started the first Southern 500 in 1950, but when all was said and done, Californian Johnny Mantz walked away the winner. Not only was it the first 500-mile race, but it was also held at the first NASCAR superspeedway – and it was paved! Note the missing headlight on the front of the car.

During the early years of Darlington, there was no wall separating the race track from the pits. In the inaugural Southern 500, Pee Wee Martin (#34 Olds) gets service and Hershel McGriff (#52 Olds) passes close by while the trio of Chuck Mahoney (#77 Mercury), pole-winner Curtis Turner (#41 Olds) and Bill Rexford (#59 Olds) run side by side.

"Well, there's sure something going on out there," Grandmother said.

"So we all got in Grandfather's big, black car and drove west to the farm. Indeed, there was something going on. Earthmovers, bulldozers and huge dump trucks were busily digging up the eastern end of the land.

"My grandfather had evidently forgotten his cursory 'sure' to Mr. Brasington, who, on Grandfather's word, had gone ahead with building the Darlington Raceway. Grandfather chuckled when he saw what was going on."

Brown said he does not know exactly what happened next. Legal matters and business dealings followed.

"Grandfather leased the land to Brasington for 99 years, formed the Darlington Raceway Corporation and became Chairman of the Board."

Brown said the dirt portion of the track was completed later in the year and the pavement was applied some time after that. During the winter, motorcycle races were held on the track, but proved too dangerous and cycle racing was quickly abandoned.

"Then came the running of the Southern 500," says Brown, "on Labor Day 1950, possibly because, in part, the conception of such a race track had occurred on the Saturday preceding Labor Day the year before."

Actually, the Labor Day Weekend was an excellent choice of dates because that particular weekend is now unofficially recognized throughout the country as the end of the summer.

One of the two biggest obstacles Harold and friends faced in building the race track was money, but Harold had reached a point in fulfilling his dream where money, or the lack of it, was not going to stop him. The other obstacle was a little more difficult because Sherman Ramsey had placed only one restriction on his deal for the land.

"I believe the original piece of the land we had was about 100 acres," recalled Harold, "but Sherman told me we couldn't destroy a fish pond that was part of that property. Over the years, people referred to it as a minnow pond. All I remember is we had to save the pond. And, we did!

"To save the pond, we had to build the first and second turns (which became Darlington Raceway's third and fourth to accommodate expansion in 1997) a little tighter than the third and fourth turns (now the first and second turns)," said Brasington. "Drivers have always said Darlington raceway is the toughest in the world, and I suppose that's because of Sherman Ramsey's fish pond." (The pond remains in place today, just beyond the new Pearson Tower seats located on the western end of the track.)

Brasington said even though many people thought his track was a hit-or-miss proposition, "It was pretty well planned out. Paul Psillos was the engineer and Gene Willis helped me with construction. Paul drew up the plans and we went to work."

Finishing the track was no easy task as Brasington kept running out of money. Ramsey had furnished the land and Darlington native R.E. (Bob) Colvin was providing some capital, but more stock had to be sold in order to complete the facility.

"Nobody but Ramsey, Colvin and Barney Wallace were interested in the project until it was about done, so stock was hard to sell," recalled Brasington. "Stock was easier to sell after the track was built and we had run that first race. When tickets for that first race started selling beyond anybody's expectations, people began to take an interest in the stock."

The track itself took shape by the end of September 1949.

Before a driver was able to talk to his crew via two-way radio communications, teams used pit boards to get messages to their drivers. Here, Maurice Petty lets his brother Richard know of a possible problem with a tire.

"I remember riding by there at night," says Harold King, "and you could see the headlights on some big equipment. Harold Brasington was not going to be denied building his race track. One cute thing I remember is how Harold's wife, Mildred, put a stop to him working at the track during the day on Sundays. Her Baptist preacher said something to her about Harold out there working on the Sabbath, and Harold didn't work at the track during the day on Sundays anymore. That's probably when he started working on the track at night."

The original dimensions of the egg-shaped track were unlike any other in existence at the time. The track was 1.25 miles around. The two straightaways were each 1,566 feet long and 85 feet wide. The turns were banked 14 degrees and were 90 feet wide, although the biggest portions of the turns were what they called the safety apron.

Time trials for the very first Labor Day Southern 500 race were held over the course of 15 days, starting August 19 and ending Saturday, September 2. The system used for qualifying was similar to that used for the Indianapolis 500, with the cars posting the five fastest times on the first day of qualifying to start on the pole through fifth positions, the fastest five from the second day in positions six through 10, and so forth. This gave Brasington and his promoters more opportunities to publicize the first 500-mile, strictly-stock automobile race.

Curtis Turner started from the pole position, even though he was not the fastest qualifier for the race. Turner averaged 82.034 mph in an Oldsmobile, but Wally Campbell posted the fastest qualifying run of the 15 days in another Oldsmobile with an average speed of 82.400.

In all, counting Turner and Campbell, 12 of the 75 cars that started the first Southern 500 averaged more than 80 miles per hour in four-lap time trials, including "Gober" Sosebee (Olds), Bob Flock (Olds), Red Byron (Cadillac), Fonty Flock (Olds), Tim Flock (Olds), Marshall Teague (Lincoln), Hershel McGriff (Olds), "Pee Wee" Martin (Olds), "Roscoe" Thompson (Olds) and Jack Carr (Mercury). There were 12 different makes of cars. The first Southern 500 starting field consisted of 29 Oldsmobiles, 10 Lincolns, seven Fords, seven Mercuries, nine Plymouths, three Hudsons, three Studebakers, two Cadillacs, two Buicks, one Pontiac, one Nash and one Kaiser.

In an ironic twist, the car posting the slowest qualifying speed of 75 starters wound up winning the race. Of course, that car was the little black No. 98Jr. Plymouth, driven by Californian Johnny Mantz. Technically, Mantz wasn't the slowest starter in the field. That distinction belonged to young driver Jesse James Taylor from Macon, Ga., who started that first Southern 500 in last place, without posting a time trial speed at all.

Cotton Owens remembers the start of the first race.

The AAA Indy cars ran at Darlington four times, including 1950. Johnny Parsons won that particular event. Here, the cars go three abreast before the start.

"We didn't really know what to expect," he says. "None of us had ever been on a track like Darlington, with the banked turns and all. The start wasn't that much different than the starts we were accustomed to on dirt tracks. There was dust and dirt flying everywhere and you could hardly see where you were going. But that wasn't any different from what we were used to. And there wasn't a big pileup down there in the first turn like we sort of expected.

"It was tough on tires, though. Man, did that place eat up the tires!"

Owens started the race in 38th position. He finished seventh, the top finish for a Palmetto State native, and he also led the race for a period of time.

Johnny Mantz, having driven in the Indianapolis 500 numerous times, knew more of what to expect in a 500-mile race on the big track. Mantz used special hard compound truck tires, similar to what they used at Indianapolis, which provided him an advantage when others were wearing tires out just about as fast as they put them on their cars. His pit crew, it was also reported, used a pneumatic lug wrench to change tires, while everyone else used standard lug wrenches.

Even Mantz' car bore a similarity to Indianapolis racing. He used the number 98Jr. on his car, which was the number he used when driving for longtime Indy car owner J.C. Agajanian from Los Angeles.

Cary Agajanian, J.C.'s son, recalls, "They asked Johnny what number he wanted on the car and he told them why not put '98Jr.' on it? Not many people know to this day the insight on why that little Plymouth carried the 98Jr. number."

NASCAR's first champion, Red Byron (winner of the inaugural 1949 NASCAR Grand National points championship, today known as the NASCAR Winston Cup Series), shed 24 tires during the race, but finished third nonetheless, behind another driver who would ultimately become a household name in NASCAR circles, Glen (Fireball) Roberts, from Daytona Beach, Fla.

Mantz actually decimated the competition in that first race, winning by nine laps – a distance of a little more than 11 miles. His average speed for the 500 miles was actually faster than his time-trial speed. He averaged 73.460 mph in qualifying and wound up running the 500 miles at an average speed of 75.250 mph.

"Man, you never saw such a bunch of cars on one race track," says Jack Smith, who was also in that first race. "It was something to see, especially from where I was sitting."

Smith started the first Southern 500 in 13th position and wound up 29th after being involved in a multi-car accident. "The tires wore out so fast, and when they did, they just blew out," recalled Smith. "There wasn't that much you could do except hold on and hope you didn't hit anything."

The race actually started at 11 a.m., the same time the Indianapolis 500 used to start when it was held on Memorial Day. The race ended a little after 6:30 p.m. (The time of the race was actually six hours, 38 minutes and 40.26 seconds.)

Harold King says the race was the most exciting thing he had ever seen.

"It seemed like it lasted a couple of days," says King with a laugh, "but the folks who came never complained about the time, the heat, running out of everything at the conces-

The Indy cars were a sight to see at Darlington.

sion stands, long lines at the restrooms, or anything else. I guess they didn't know any better.

"I mean, we had nothing to compare it to back then. We only had one hotel in town, so people in Darlington opened up their homes to the drivers and teams, and the fans. It was a festive occasion, a fun occasion, and folks around Darlington had never seen the likes of it.

"One of the things I remember the most is how everybody lined the square in downtown Darlington after the race was over. It seemed like you saw a little bit of everything after all those people came roaring through town on their way back home."

Estimates on attendance reached as high as 25,000 spectators, more than twice the number of people Brasington, Bill France and others had expected.

"We don't know how many people were there," said Harold Brasington, "because once we sold all the reserved seat tickets and we didn't have any room for more people in the infield, fans just tore the fences down and came on in anyway."

While Johnny Mantz might have left the tough, old track in a happy mood, Cotton Owens and others just like him weren't so fortunate. "When the race was over and everybody was heading home, we had to find a garage we could rent or borrow so we could fix the car in order to be able to drive it back home. I think a local fellow was kind enough to loan us his garage and we fixed [the car]. There were plenty of others who didn't drive their cars home. They were too torn up."

Other memories of that first Southern 500? Well, the women wore their finest, Sunday-best outfits, because no one knew what to expect. The tire dust ruined many pretty dresses, and it didn't take the women long to figure out they needed wide-brimmed hats to shield the Labor Day sun.

There were a couple of other things standard in those days, which wouldn't make much sense in today's NASCAR environment. The flagman started the race from trackside, meaning down on the race track (That had to be a thrill of thrills!), and pit crews were not shielded by a wall between them and the cars on the track.

When drivers needed to stop for tires or gas during that first Southern 500, they simply slowed down, came down on the apron of the track and stopped alongside the inside retaining wall. Their crews jumped over the fence and serviced the cars while, 20 or 30 feet away, the race was continuing with nothing in between.

It was sort of "learn as you go" for both Darlington Raceway and NASCAR, as well as the drivers, car owners, teams and fans. By today's standards, like many other things, it was primitive. Fans slept on the Courthouse grounds in the middle of downtown. The Darlington Jaycees kept a hot dog stand open all night before the big race, and people were milling around. Excitement was in the air, and no one wanted to sleep. Strangers became friends. As Harold King put it, "The old adrenaline got to flowing like a flash-flood of anticipation!"

And speaking of primitive, think about this: During that first Southern 500, the only communication between drivers and crews were "pit boards," like schoolhouse chalkboards. A mechanic would write signals on the blackboard and hold it up for the driver to read as he sped by his location in the pits.

Some of the signals crews would give their drivers were: PIT (this meant to stop); EZ (take it easy, you're running the car too hard); 5TH, No. 11 4TH (you're running in fifth

position and car No. 11 is in fourth ahead of you); $$$$$ (many times, crews would put dollar signs on the pit board to flash to the driver after he had crossed the start-finish line to win a race); TIRES? (Crews would ask drivers if their tires were okay and drivers would signal as they came back the next lap. If the tires weren't okay, the drivers usually would pull in the pits unexpectedly or blow a tire and hit something. (There were no inner liners for stock cars until 1964, so when a driver said he "blowed a tire," he literally had a blowout – the cause of numerous crashes at Darlington in the first few years.)

Actually, the track had to have been tougher to drive than it is today due to changes in technology such as better tires, more horsepower, padded seats, bigger windshields, roll cages, better aerodynamics, driving uniforms and driving shoes, just to mention a few of the improvements made in 50 years.

Brasington, however, always said his track would not only be a test of the drivers. "It would be an endurance test for family sedans – a way of proving which American make of car was the best – for 500 miles, anyway."

Brasington's belief played right into the hands of Bill France and his National Association for Stock Car Auto Racing, newly-formed in 1949. It was France who answered the call from Brasington when he found himself in trouble with entries for that first race a few months before the event. Brasington had made an arrangement with the CSRA (Central States Racing Association) to sanction his first Southern 500. (There were many new sanctioning organizations to choose from at the time, if a promoter was looking for someone to handle the actual running of the event.)

Brasington chose CSRA simply because Harold and Bill France had been unable to get together, and Brasington needed a sanctioning organization. When Brasington called and told France the CSRA was having trouble getting entries, Bill told Harold not to worry, "We'll get the entries for you."

In six career Southern 500 starts from 1951-56, Herb Thomas won three times and finished in the top five in two of the other events.

France not only got the entries, but also came up with the idea to open the infield the night before the race because the people lining up to get in were clogging the local highways.

"We let them in the night before and then asked everybody to go back outside the next morning to buy a ticket," said Brasington. "And, they did."

The first Southern 500 at the new Darlington Raceway was not the only race at the track that first year. Brasington also scheduled motorcycles and Indy cars, but neither was successful. Actually, the only motorcycle race ever scheduled was not completed. Two motorcyclists were killed in preliminary events, forcing a cancellation. The Indy cars simply didn't draw spectators, even though some of the biggest stars of the Indianapolis 500 showed up to race, such as Johnny Parsons and Bill Holland, former winners of the Indianapolis 500.

By Labor Day 1951, the racing world once again focused on Darlington, S.C. NASCAR was on its way, and this event was the focus of the season since it was the only 500-mile race on the schedule.

The 1951 event featured the biggest names in stock car racing, including Herb Thomas, Cotton Owens, Jim Paschal, Buck Baker, Curtis Turner, Fireball Roberts, Fonty Flock, Tim Flock, Frank Mundy, Red Byron, Buddy Shuman, Marshall Teague, Iggy Katona (who later made a name for himself in the Automobile Racing Club of America, known today as ARCA), Hershel McGriff, a young Californian who won the Mexican road race with Bill France Sr., Gober Sosebee, Billy Myers, Lee Petty and Gwyn Staley (whose brother, Enoch Staley, became one of NASCAR's most dedicated promoters and eventually built North Wilkesboro Speedway).

One of the most interesting things about the 1951 Southern 500 is that a Studebaker won the pole position.

(Above) Victory lane was a little bit different back in 1951 than it is today. Fans swarm around Herb Thomas' Fabulous Hudson Hornet after he captured his first of three Southern 500 triumphs.

(Right) After winning the 1951 Southern 500, Herb Thomas is congratulated by his car owner, Marshall Teague, while the Raceway's Harold Brasington (left) and Bob Colvin (right) look on.

Most readers would ask, "What was a Studebaker?" Well, the best way to describe it is a sporty-looking little American-made passenger car that most folks regarded as a pretty reliable piece of transportation, but not exactly what you would want under you if sheer power and speed was the goal.

Nonetheless, Frank (Rebel) Mundy mustered enough speed to put the little car on the coveted pole with a record speed of 84.173 mph. Once again, the pole winner did not have the overall fastest qualifying speed, but was the fastest on the first day of time trials.

The fastest car in time trials belonged to Marshall Teague (87.636 mph), who was one of six drivers in a Hudson Hornet, a "fastback" model of its day that was also a "step-down" model, meaning the floorboard was well below the door – more so than any other make of car. The Hudson Hornet was also factory backed, and many people think of the "Fabulous Hudson Hornet" as the first factory-backed brand in NASCAR. (Hudsons won 79 NASCAR Grand National races before a company merger did away with the brand.)

A Hudson Hornet with Herb Thomas at the wheel won the 1951 Southern 500, and another Hudson with young Jesse James Taylor driving finished second. (Taylor was hurt later in the season and his injuries were serious enough to thwart a promising career.) Thomas, a former sawmill operator, trucker and farmer from Olivia, N.C., drove the No. 92 Hudson with the "Fabulous Hudson Hornet" factory slogan emblazoned on the car to a one-lap victory in six hours, 30 minutes and five seconds. (This car is now on permanent display at the National Motorsports

On his way to a victory in the 1952 Southern 500, Fonty Flock (#14) gets ready to pass Donald Thomas (#66) on the front straightaway. Note the public address speakers on top of one of racing's first VIP Suites.

Press Association Hall of Fame Museum located at Darlington Raceway, as is the No. 98Jr. Plymouth driven to victory by Johnny Mantz in the first Southern 500.)

"The second race went a lot smoother than the first," said Harold Brasington, who had relegated most of the responsibilities of operating the race track to Robert E. (Bob) Colvin.

Unfortunately, Uncle Sam came looking for Harold and he had to sell his stock to settle tax debts. "I was always good at building things," said Harold years later. "Running them and doing all the things you have to do just wasn't for me. I wasn't a detail person, and the books sort of pointed that out when the IRS came in. I owed all this money for taxes so I had to sell what stock I had to settle up."

The 1952 Darlington Southern 500 would not be the first time fans would see NASCAR Grand National cars race at Darlington that year. NASCAR's Grand National Division actually ran twice that year, the first time in May as a support race for NASCAR's struggling Speedway Division – Indianapolis cars with stock motors.

There was actually a shortage of Speedway (Indy) cars, so NASCAR's Grand National circuit was hustled to Darlington as a "save-face" measure. Dick Rathman won the hastily-scheduled race in a Hudson Hornet, with the Flock brothers – Tim and Fonty – finishing second and third, respectively. Tim drove a Hudson while Fonty was in an Oldsmobile.

The 1952 race was also a first of another kind. It was the first time "Little" Joe Weatherly from Norfolk, Va., one of the nation's best motorcycle riders, would compete at Darlington. And, believe it or not, he was driving a Hudson Hornet prepared by none other than Junie Donlavey, who would become one of NASCAR's most popular chief mechanics and car owners in the years to come.

Fontello (Fonty) Flock, one of the most colorful drivers in NASCAR history, won the 1952 Southern 500 driving an Oldsmobile, and Hudson Hornets captured the next four positions with Johnny Patterson, Herb Thomas, "Bub" King and Edwin "Banjo" Matthews at the wheel.

Lee Petty's Plymouth was sixth, and Weatherly, in his first Darlington race, finished 16th. Only 66 cars started this one, but 39 of the 66 were still running when the race finished six hours, 42 minutes and 37 seconds later.

The colorful Flock played to the fans in victory lane, leading them in a rousing rendition of "Dixie," which, at the time, was a popular song amongst the southern masses. Flock not only led the singing from atop the roof of his winning car, but the fans could also see that he had driven the race wearing a pair of stylish (at the time) Bermuda shorts. Some folks would say this was NASCAR's first venture into fashion wear. Others would say it was Flock's version of a "cool suit" to thwart the heat generated inside a speeding passenger car for 400 laps around the tough, old Darlington Raceway.

Actually, from a historical standpoint, it was the first time in Darlington history that the pole-position winner wound up in victory lane. Flock earned the pole with a qualifying speed of 88.55 mph. (Advertising pundits and headline writers should have had a field day with Flock driving an Oldsmobile, which was known as the Olds 88 or the Rocket Olds. Can't you just see the headline? FLOCK ROCKETS TO 88 MPH IN HIS OLDS 88!)

Even though his Rocket Olds was fast, Fonty's average speed for the 500 miles at Darlington was the slowest to date (74.512 mph). It took him six hours, 42 minutes and 37 seconds to win the race.

Just to get a clear understanding of what these street-stock NASCAR race cars were like in the 1950s, consider this: These cars raced with their headlights and tail lights intact, with some tape over them. They sometimes didn't remove the glass. The chrome fixtures on the hood and trunk remained in place. The shiny, chrome-covered front and rear bumpers were a cumbersome, separate part of the cars, just like the ones on the roads, and these parts were designed to protect the rest of the car in case of an accident. The phrase, "Put a bumper on 'em!" literally meant what it implied.

Most of the cars had AM radios, and you sometimes could detect the radio antenna protruding from a race car. Some of the cars also had their windshield wipers intact. (The wiper blades might be removed for the race because stock cars didn't race in the rain, but they needed the windshield wipers for driving the cars back home after the race.)

(Top) In 1952, Fonty Flock (right) won his only Southern 500 at Darlington. The Raceway's Bob Colvin (left) and NASCAR's Bill France make a presentation to Flock. That's South Carolina Governor Strom Thurmond behind the microphone.

(Left) When Buck Baker (left) and Joe Weatherly (right) weren't racing, they were fishing with former Darlington Raceway President Bob Colvin (center).

There were no roll cages as we know them today. The cars of yesterday were built solid with plenty of steel underneath the paint. The handles to roll the windows up and down were still in the cars, as well as handles to open and shut the doors. Gas tanks were standard also. There were no such things as fuel cells at the time.

Most of the cars had one seat all the way across the front of the car, since bucket seats had not become standard equipment, and there were "Oh, Shoot! Hold On!" handles attached to the back of the front seat so passengers had something to grab on to in sudden stops or bumpy rides. These race cars also had glove boxes; in fact, the cars also had speedometers, and all the other standard passenger-car gauges. The dashboards, as the instrument panels were called in those days, were intact, for the most part.

By 1953, Darlington Raceway's reputation was growing, and Robert E. (Bob) Colvin was gaining notoriety as a promoter. This native of Darlington was a successful peanut broker with plenty of charisma. The cigar-chewing, story-telling, back-slapping, grinning, bald-headed Colvin was everybody's favorite, and he did as much as anyone in those formative years to boost stock car racing's popularity and respectability.

Colvin traveled extensively throughout the Carolinas, developed friendships in Virginia, and ventured south into Georgia and Northern Florida, hanging posters, visiting newspaper sports departments and radio stations, and telling anyone who would listen that they needed to be in Darlington for the "greatest stock car race in the world, the Southern 500."

Posters were a big part of advertising the Southern 500 in those early days. They were stapled onto telephone poles alongside highly traveled routes and put in the windows of grocery stores gracious enough to allow it. A few complimentary tickets to the Southern 500 went, as Colvin put it, "a long, long way in gaining window space."

Colvin's persuasive personality accounted for many mentions on radio and many lines in sports sections for a sport that was desperately trying to gain acceptability and some degree of respectability, compared to the more traditional sports such as baseball, football and basketball.

Between Big Bill France on a national level and Bob Colvin on a regional level, NASCAR and Darlington Raceway had two of America's premier salesmen spreading the word. As one sportswriter put it, "If either one of those two ever had the opportunity to sit down with you one-on-one, you'd wind up buying whatever it was they were selling."

Former Darlington Raceway President Bob Colvin (left) talks with Ralph Pond about the paving process of the track in 1953. Turns one and two were completely reworked to increase the banking, which, in turn, increased speeds.

NMPA Hall of Famer Fonty Flock, who won the 1952 Southern 500, was famous for wearing his Bermuda shorts while behind the wheel.

Colvin, for his part, was selling Darlington. And he became a fixture at many of NASCAR's other races, making sure drivers and car owners were planning to participate in the Southern 500. It was common practice then for promoters to attend other events for the purpose of getting drivers to sign entry blanks for their upcoming races, so they could publicize which drivers planned to participate in their particular race.

If Colvin was in attendance at an event, the word spread rapidly, because many of the competitors enjoyed picking at him and playing practical jokes on him. It was common practice to see a driver sneak up behind Colvin and touch him in the ribs, which would prompt him to jump and yell out a string of obscenities (Colvin was goosey, as they would say) to the laughing delight of the driver or mechanic who triggered the incident. Bob Colvin was universally popular with competitors and members of the press, and became, along with Virginia promoter Paul Sawyer, a close personal friend of Joe Weatherly.

Terry Josey has been a staunch supporter of Darlington Raceway since its inception, and Josey says Colvin's intelligence, as well as his personality, kept the fledgling track above water in the early going.

"Colvin was amazing," says Terry, a Darlington native who helped out around the track from the very beginning. "I remember a couple of things that happened for the first Southern 500 that, if it hadn't been for Colvin, several items would have been completely forgotten. Actually, they were forgotten until Colvin brought them up. The first item was insurance. I remember Colvin asking about insurance either the day before or the day of the race, and then getting on the phone with somebody at K&K Insurance. The track wouldn't have had any insurance if he hadn't thought of it.

"Another thing was wreckers, which no one thought of for that first race. Colvin said on race morning, or maybe it was the day before, that they needed to have some wreckers here to haul race cars if they crash. He called Mott Pierce, and Mott handled the wreckers at the track for a number of years. Mott was another one of the local folks who enjoyed racing and always supported the track."

Colvin appreciated the support of the local people and was always generous in the track's support of civic projects.

The Raceway president organized a fund-raiser to purchase the first band uniforms in St. John's (Darlington) High School history. He also organized a trip for the members of the school patrol, which became one of the most sought-after prizes in Darlington by elementary school students. The trip consisted of a couple of days in Daytona Beach, Fla., cookouts and side trips to tourist attractions such as Silver Springs, home of the world-famous glass-bottom boats. (Disney World, Sea World and Cape Canaveral did not become Florida tourist destinations until many years later.) The Raceway and the Darlington Police Department co-sponsored this effort for many years.

Colvin was also very active in the Darlington Lion's

The fans in the infield, as well as the pit crews behind the pit wall, anticipate the start of the 1954 Southern 500 at Darlington Raceway.

Club, and was a staunch supporter of his alma mater, Clemson University, where he received an engineering degree.

In 1953, while Colvin, Vice-President Barney Wallace, another local native who loved stock car racing, Walter D. (Red) Tyler and others were preparing the Raceway for its fourth annual Southern 500, Hudson Hornets were winning 18 of 29 races leading up to Darlington.

With that in mind, it came as no great surprise that Fonty Flock put his Hornet on the pole for the race. Sixteen of the 59 starters in the race drove Hudsons, including former winners Flock and Thomas, as well as Dick Rathman, who had won four races leading up the

Southern 500. Needless to say, the Hudsons were heavy favorites.

The race wound up being what many fans at the time considered to be the most competitive race in NASCAR's short history. Four drivers, two in Hudsons and two in Olds 88s, swapped the lead 35 times on the newly-revamped 1.375-mile track. (The distance had been somewhat lengthened when turns one and two were repaved.) Buck Baker and Fireball Roberts dueled with Fonty Flock and Herb Thomas throughout the 364-lap race before Baker passed Thomas just 10 laps from the finish to take the win.

Thomas had a slight lead over Baker heading into the race's final stages, but his Hornet suffered engine failure

Fireball Roberts makes an unscheduled pit stop at Darlington.

and Baker zipped past. Fellow Hudson driver Gene Comstock pushed Thomas around the track until the checkered flag fell over Baker's car, but Thomas was relegated to a fifth-place finish when NASCAR disallowed the two laps made courtesy of Comstock's push.

Baker's Oldsmobile averaged 92.881 miles per hour in covering the 500 miles in five hours, 23 minutes and 19 seconds. While Baker did not start first, his Oldsmobile was the first entry for the event, rolling right out of the showroom at Griffin Motors in nearby Florence, S.C., to the NASCAR inspection station near the track.

Terry Josey remembers the old inspection station – the one Cotton Owens remembered as being "just down the road from the track."

"The inspection place was actually Bill Bryant's garage," said Josey, whose son, Mac Josey, is now the track's operations manager. "Bill Bryant was the sheriff of Darlington County back then, and he had this little old garage there at his house. It was made out of block with a tin roof on it,

and it sort of looks like a barn. Back then, it really looked like a barn. (The first NASCAR/Darlington inspection station still stands and is located four miles west of the Raceway off Highway 151.)

"The inspection place wasn't used all that much until after the races, but different drivers used Bryant's place to work on their cars, just like they used Mr. Bill Garland's place in town (downtown Darlington off East Main Street near where the IGA store is today)."

Josey says he remembers how the cars would have to put the mufflers back on when they left the race track. "The guys would bolt the mufflers back on or tie them back on, take the tape off the headlights and taillights, and drive them right out of the track. People don't believe you when you tell them that today. But that's the way it was.

"I remember one of those early races (1954), when Darlington and NASCAR were short on race cars. Bob Colvin put his wife's Oldsmobile in the race, and he put Speedy Thompson's brother, Jimmy Thompson, in his wife's car for the race.

"Bob's wife (Loomis) didn't like it at all, but that's the way Colvin was. He figured if Thompson tore it up, he'd get it fixed or get her another car. That car was a pretty good car, though, because I wound up buying it. It was a green '54 Olds."

Thompson qualified Loomis Colvin's Oldsmobile 36th, but fell out after just a few laps and finished dead last. The official reason for leaving the race was listed as "fuel tank," but it is likely the real reason was that Bob Colvin was afraid Jimmy Thompson would tear up his wife's car, so he instructed Thompson to take the starting flag and park it after a few laps. Thompson was actually credited with four complete laps in the race.

Seventy-five cars started the first Southern 500. Eighty-two started the second, 66 started the third, 59 started the fourth and only 50 started in 1954, but that 1954 race was a humdinger! Herb Thomas zoomed past Curtis Turner at the 475-mile point of the race to give the Hudson Hornet fans their second Southern 500 victory. It would also be Hudson's last Southern 500 win.

The race itself was ultra-competitive with Thomas and Turner swapping the lead for the final half of the race before Thomas charged home the winner. Finishing third behind Turner's Oldsmobile was Marvin Panch in a Dodge. Johnny Patterson was fourth in a Mercury, and Jim Paschal, one of the sport's future stars, was fifth in another Oldsmobile.

The view from the press box over the frontstretch grandstand was breathtaking. Most fans couldn't stay off their feet.

Other drivers who would eventually play a big part in the growth of the sport were also in the 1954 Southern 500, including Fireball Roberts, who finished 7th. Gwynn Staley, brother of longtime NASCAR official Enoch Staley, a pioneer promoter in the sport who founded and ran North Wilkesboro Speedway until his death in 1995, finished 8th. In 12th place was Elmo Langley, one of NASCAR's most enthusiast and well-liked drivers who eventually became NASCAR's official pace-car driver. Cotton Owens finished 34th, Lee Petty 38th, Buck Baker 44th and Hershel McGriff finished in 45th place. McGriff won the first Pan-American Road Race in 1950, a 2,135-mile event with Bill France Sr. as his co-driver, and later became a NASCAR Winston West Series superstar, racing competitively well into his 60s. McGriff won four NASCAR Winston Cup Series races, including two during the 1954 season at the half-mile dirt track in Macon, Georgia.

McGriff, one of the most personable drivers in the history of the sport, might have made history the next year had he not turned down an offer to become a "team" driver for Karl Kiekhafer's Chrysler team. Kiekhafer, owner of the Mercury Marine Corporation that manufactured outboard motors, decided to use NASCAR Grand National racing as a means of advertising his products. McGriff, after Kiekhafer asked which drivers might be available to race for his team, was one of those France recommended. McGriff declined, however, and returned to the West Coast to pursue his fortune in the lumber business. McGriff returned to racing many years later in the NASCAR

Winston West Series, but never looked back at what might have been.

By the time the 1955 Southern 500 rolled around, Kiekhafer was the talk of the circuit. He had burst on the scene, and his independently-owned Chryslers, with their big, powerful engines and piloted by a stable of the best drivers in the business, were changing the entire face of NASCAR racing.

Kiekhafer, for his limited days in the sport, made stock car racing a science. His crews wore uniforms rather than coveralls. His cars, even when racing on dirt, were polished and clean. He had his teams analyze everything – from the type and texture of the dirt at each race track, to the effect of prevalent temperature and relative humidity on the tuning of the engines, and anything else that might give them an edge on the competition.

Some of the stories repeated over the years even mentioned rules such as "no drinking, no cussing, no carousing, and early to bed – early to rise" for Kiekhafer's personnel, including his drivers. But those stories might have been more fiction than fact when one considers the list of those who drove his cars, including fun-loving Fonty Flock and Buck Baker, a free-wheeling spirit who lived and drove by his own rules.

When Bob Colvin and the rest of the Darlington gang began making preparations for the 1955 Southern 500, Kiekhafer's operation was on everyone's mind. Tim Flock, whose No. 300 Kiekhafer Chrysler carried the slogan "Mercury Outboards, The Most Powerful Name In Outboards," had established the Kiekhafer name by winning the first big race of that year on the old Daytona

Birds-eye view. In the early years of Darlington Raceway, a pedestrian crossover existed over the old backstretch. It was later removed.

The crowd waited to see Herb Thomas in victory lane after his 1955 Southern 500 victory.

Beach road course, although Fireball Roberts had been flagged the winner. Flock finished second, but was awarded the victory when Roberts' car was found to be "technically" illegal. (Ironically, Flock had won the same race the year before, but was disqualified in a post-race inspection and didn't race with NASCAR for the rest of the 1954 season.)

From the beginning of the 1955 season, Flock, in the Kiekhafer Chrysler, was "The Man." He won 12 of 34 races coming into the Southern 500 and had clearly established his car as one of the favorites in the Labor Day classic.

Flock and the Kiekhafer team, which, by Darlington, was a two-car operation that included Tim's brother Fonty, prompted much attention. The race would also mark the return of crowd favorite Herb Thomas, a two-time winner of the Southern 500 who had been hospitalized for several months while recovering from injuries he received during an accident at Charlotte.

Darlington's Southern 500, in just a few short years, had become what Brasington and Bill France had envisioned. It drew national attention to the sport that crisscrossed the country, staging races on quarter-mile ovals and half-mile bullrings from Arizona to New York. The Southern 500 had become THE stock car race. This was the event all drivers and car owners wanted to win.

With that in mind, this was the first reported sellout for stock car racing, with reports circulating that all 50,000 printed tickets were sold 24 hours prior to the race. By stock car standards, the crowd at Darlington for the 1955 Southern 500 was very likely the largest crowd to see a stock car event that year.

Sixty-nine cars qualified for the race, with Fireball Roberts winning the pole in a Buick at an average speed of 110.682 mph. Tim Flock actually had the fastest car in the race with a time-trial speed of more than 112 mph, but Roberts was fastest on the first day of qualifying. The race itself was a dandy, with Roberts, both Flock boys, Curtis

Turner, Bill Widenhouse, Joe Weatherly and Thomas all charging to the front. But tire problems and accidents posed problems for everyone except Thomas, who put a storybook finish on the race with a victory in his first appearance since being hurt, his third Southern 500 triumph.

New Yorker Jim Reed was second behind Thomas, giving Chevrolet a 1-2 finish, with Tim Flock crossing the line third. Rounding out the top 10 were Gwyn Staley (Chevrolet), Larry Flynn (Ford), Buck Baker (Buick), Lou Spear (Chevrolet), Cotton Owens (Chevrolet), Bill Widenhouse (Chevrolet) and Jimmy Massey (Chevrolet).

Bob Colvin is one of those folks who never let any grass grow under his feet. He was always thinking of ways to improve the track, and by 1956, Darlington Raceway was improving. The track was adding reserved seats, and Colvin tore down the old crossover bridge and built the first of two tunnels for traffic getting into and out of the Raceway. He also tore down the old infield pagoda and erected a new control tower. With the cooperation of NASCAR, Colvin installed pits along the backstretch to accommodate the tremendous number of cars running in the Southern 500.

In those days, the cars were not allowed to pit during caution periods because there was no way that 50, 60 or 70 cars would all have space to pit at the same time. In addition, the old pagoda had been built so that cars coming into the pits had to make a little zig-zag to go around it – not exactly what one would call the perfect pit area. But everything was based on a learning curve back then, and the new tower eliminated the zig-zag problem, making things much better for the drivers and crews.

Reserved-seat tickets to the 1955 Southern 500 cost $6, $8 and $10, with the most expensive seats being closest to

The 1956 Southern 500 was Herb Thomas' last run at Darlington. As you can see by his battered machine, his day wasn't a good one. He finished 49th.

the track, called "box seats." The total purse was $40,000, whereas the purses for most of the short-track races were less than $4,000. Fans could buy R.C. Cola at the concession stand for 15 cents. Milk was 25 cents. A cold beer was 30 cents. Hotdogs sold for a quarter, and a fried-ham sandwich cost twice that much. Cigarettes were 35 cents a pack. Ice for an ice chest was a whopping $1.50, and it was hard to keep enough ice on hand with the humid Labor Day weather.

An even bigger crowd turned out for the 1956 race to watch Herb Thomas gun for his fourth Southern 500 victory. Favorites included Buck Baker, Fireball Roberts, Joe Weatherly and Speedy Thompson, along with the Flock boys in their Kiekhafer Chryslers. Another pre-race avorite was Curtis Turner, who had led each of the previous Southern 500s, but had yet to win. This race, however, was all Turner's as he dominated the 500 miles in his purple Ford.

The Kiekhafer Chryslers once again failed to win the biggest race of the year, although Speedy Thompson drove one of Kiekhafer's cars to second place. Marvin Panch was third in a Ford followed by Jim Reed in a Chevy. Rookie Paul Goldsmith from St. Clair Shores, Mich., was fifth in a Smokey Yunick-prepared Chevrolet. Goldsmith, a national champion motorcycle racer, became one of NASCAR's top stars after this sterling debut at the circuit's toughest track.

Other Kiekhafer cars fared poorly, with Buck Baker 26th and Rebel Mundy 38th. Dick Beaty, an aspiring young driver from Charlotte, N.C., who would later become a top NASCAR official, wound up 40th after a grinding accident that destroyed his Ford. Thomas, Roberts, and Ralph Moody also were eliminated from competition in crashes, as was future Indianapolis driving sensation Parnelli Jones.

Darlington Raceway's 1957 season is remembered by many as being the most eventful since 1950. It certainly was newsworthy.

The Miss Southern 500 Beauty Pageant (It was okay to refer to a Beauty Pageant as a Beauty Pageant in those days; today, the terminology has changed to Scholarship

Pageant.) was joined by the Southern 500 Parade as a preliminary event leading up to the race itself.

The Pageant, now in its fifth year, had established itself from its inception when Martha Dean Chestnut of Conway, S.C., won the first one and went on to become Miss South Carolina. The brainchild of Bob Colvin, the Miss Southern 500 Beauty Pageant has remained a springboard for college scholarships to hundreds of young South Carolina women who compete for the Miss Southern 500 title as a preliminary event to the Miss South Carolina Scholarship Pageant.

In 1957, as it had been in previous years, the Pageant was held on the Raceway's frontstretch the Saturday night

(Right) Curtis Turner was a two-time winner at Darlington – the 1956 Southern 500 and the 1958 Rebel 300 for the NASCAR Convertible Series.

(Below) Doug Yates (#25) gets into the back of Gwyn Staley (#2) during the 1956 Southern 500. Both drivers were done for the day while Ralph Moody (#12), Joe Weatherly (#9) and Lee Petty (#35) continued. Curtis Turner won the classic.

before the Southern 500. Many of the drivers served as judges for the Pageant in those days.

In the evolution of Darlington Raceway and the sport in general, there were significant changes in the competition arena during 1957. For example, NASCAR, for the first time, would allow teams to refuel during caution periods. Teams would also be allowed to use 10-gallon cans or weld two five-gallon cans together to speed up pit stops. Also for the first time, mechanics (crew members) were required to wear shirts. There was quite a bit of grumbling in the pits over this rule because of the heat and humidity, not to mention the fact that some of the crew members used Darlington's Labor Day Classic as a means of getting a tan – or a terrible sunburn.

There was another "first" at Darlington in 1957: The very first Rebel 300 was held. The race was scheduled on the second Saturday in May, celebrated by some in the South as Confederate Memorial Day, thus the "Rebel 300." It was also the first Convertible race at Darlington. (Needless to say, aerodynamics did not play a huge role in stock car racing at the time.)

NASCAR formed the

Paul Goldsmith won the pole position for the first Rebel 300 in 1957. Here, Bob Colvin makes the trophy presentation.

Convertible Division in 1956, but the Rebel 300 would be this new division's first outing on a major speedway, having staged their races on the traditional quarter-mile and half-mile tracks, as well as the bigger dirt tracks such as Hillsboro, N.C. (9/10 mile) and the one-mile ovals at Langhorne, Pa., and Syracuse, N.Y.

While many of today's drivers fly to and from race tracks, Paul Goldsmith of Griffin, Indiana, was one of the first.

Paul Goldsmith started from the pole position with a four-lap average speed of 115.320 mph in qualifying – fastest of the 27-car field that included most of the big names of the day. Fireball Roberts went on to win the race, but not until ol' Bob Colvin had thumbed his nose at South Carolina's notorious "blue laws," which prohibited most commercial activities such as stock car racing from being held on Sunday. Most ordinary places of business were closed on Sundays in South Carolina, such as grocery stores, department stores, etc.

It rained most of the day on Saturday (May 11th, 1957) so Colvin rescheduled the race for Sunday, May 12th. South Carolina's blue laws prescribed a $50 fine for anyone in violation, so Colvin paid the fine and ran the race against the wishes of many clergy in his hometown, not to mention statewide.

In fact, as Terry Josey recalls, "The preacher at Darlington's First Baptist Church, William S. Jones, told Colvin he would lie down on the track in front of the pace car to prevent the race from starting. But ol' Bob told him he'd be a dead preacher if he tried it!"

The first Convertible race at Darlington produced the biggest pileup in Darlington history when 17 of the 27 cars that started the race were involved in a chain-reaction accident on lap 29 of the 219-lap event. Among those eliminated

NASCAR's Convertible Division began Darlington Raceway's springtime tradition with the 1957 Rebel 300. As you can see, the view from the cockpit of Curtis Turner's car was spectacular. The "ragtops" competed at Darlington through 1962.

We Lead...
Others Follow

in the fiasco were Curtis Turner, Joe Weatherly, Billy Myers, Goldsmith, Marvin Panch and Buck Baker.

Roberts won by more than two laps with Tim Flock second, Bobby Myers third, Bob Welborn fourth and Lee Petty fifth.

The 1957 season at Darlington continued its historical significance when its president, Bob Colvin, began helping drivers recruit endorsements. Among them was Spartanburg native Johnny Allen, one of the hard-charging youngsters who drove with reckless abandon. Allen had an endorsement agreement with Grey-Rock, the premier brake-lining company of the time. Grey-Rock was a division of Raybestos-Manhattan Inc., and Allen recalls his lucrative endorsement consisting of "free brake linings, probably. But that was pretty big back then. At least you didn't have to buy them."

Three-time Southern 500 winner Herb Thomas was featured in Purolator print ads and Paul Goldsmith was used in a print ad for Pee Dee Motor Company in Timmonsville, S.C. Chances are that Thomas' team received free Purolator oil filters and Goldsmith didn't have to rent or borrow a car while in Darlington for the races.

Darlington Raceway had a radio network then, with Florence station WJMX handling the feed. Paul Benson, WJMX owner and general manager, started the network in 1952, and by 1957 it had grown to over 100 stations in eight states. With WJMX in Florence serving as the "home" station/producer and Benson eagerly taking on more responsi-

bilities, the Southern 500 became one of America's top 10 radio sports broadcasts.

Benson brought in very capable people from the beginning. Charles Bailey, Tancil Horne, Dave Moss and Dave Thomas were the pit reporters and color announcers, while high atop the pagoda, smooth-voiced Dave Rogers carried the play-by-play with Johnny Evans and Jack Wymer handling features in the booth.

With festivities growing every year and the race gaining more and more attention through sports pages and the Darlington Raceway Network, the buildup to the 1957 Southern 500 was spectacular.

Paul Goldsmith won the pole for the event, and the 51-car field featured favorites such as Curtis Turner, Buck Baker, Fireball Roberts, Herb Thomas, Jim Reed, Lee Petty, Joe Weatherly, Speedy Thompson, Bill Amick, Marvin Panch, Glen Wood (of the famed Wood Brothers in later years), Tiny Lund, Bob Welborn and Cotton Owens, one of NASCAR's most successful modified drivers from Spartanburg, S.C.

Thirty-three-year-old Bobby Myers of Winston-Salem, N.C., became the first Southern 500 fatality after a multi-car crash involving Myers, Fonty Flock and Paul Goldsmith on the 27th lap. Myers crashed head-on into the disabled car of Flock at the entrance to the third turn, with the impact of the crash knocking the engine out of Myers' Oldsmobile. Goldsmith also broadsided Flock's car, sending Flock to a Florence hospital for several days before being

Cruising with the top down. The starting field takes a parade lap for the 1958 Rebel 300, the second year for the NASCAR Convertible Series at Darlington.

released. Flock never drove again. Goldsmith recovered and continued racing.

When the race continued, Lee Petty and Fireball Roberts swapped the lead during the next 70 laps before Jack Smith took over the front spot in his Chevrolet. Former winner Curtis Turner charged to the front for a while, but Thompson took the lead for good on the 216th lap and held off the field the rest of the way.

Cotton Owens finished second in a Pontiac. Marvin Panch was third, Jim Reed fourth and Buck Baker fifth. Rounding out the top 10 were Billy Carden (6th), Bobby Myers' brother Billy (7th), John Mackison (8th), Possum Jones (9th) and Jack Smith (10th).

Future Indianapolis 500 winner Parnelli Jones finished 34th, and a future three-time NASCAR Winston Cup Series champion, Cale Yarborough from nearby Timmonsville, finished 42nd in his first Southern 500. One spot ahead of Cale in that race was another legend, Banjo Matthews.

Marvin Panch stands beside his convertible prior to the start of the 1958 Rebel 300.

Fireball Roberts, Marvin Panch and Cotton Owens shared the front row for the 1958 Rebel 300 NASCAR Convertible race, but Curtis Turner wound up winning it in his Ford. Roberts was Chevrolet's top finisher in the race in fifth place, which was a Ford sweep of the top-four positions with Joe Weatherly trailing Turner in second, Marvin Panch third and Eddie Pagan fourth.

Pagan's name was to become synonymous with that of Darlington Raceway because he was to survive the most horrific-looking crash in Darlington Raceway history when the 1958 Southern 500 rolled around. Pagan, from Lynwood, Calif., had put his Ford on the pole for the ninth annual running of the Southern 500 and led many of the first 135 laps, swapping the lead back and forth with Joe Weatherly, Joe Eubanks, Curtis Turner and Speedy Thompson.

Pagan's pole-winning effort was not a surprise because Eddie had been the first driver to arrive for the Darlington practice sessions and logged over 400 miles in shakedown runs. Pagan had, in fact, moved his family to Charlotte, N.C., in order to concentrate on the stock car circuit.

After 136 laps, Pagan was charging hard, running what had become known as the "Darlington Stripe" groove through turns three and four, leaning his Ford ever so slightly against the guardrail to maintain momentum through the tricky, treacherous turns that measured just over 30 feet in width. Suddenly, the right-front tire on Pagan's Ford blew, slamming him into the guardrail at full speed. His machine hit with such force, the impact ripped a gaping hole in the guardrail and Pagan's car tumbled down the outside embankment and came to rest, the Ford barely recognizable. Pagan suffered only a broken nose.

"To this day, Pagan's crash has to be one of the worst I've ever seen at Darlington," says Harold King.

NASCAR and track officials could not repair the hole in the third-turn guardrail and instructed the drivers to stay away from it. When the race resumed, fate would deal a bad Darlington hand to another Eddie, this time it was Eddie Gray. Gray's car slipped in the third turn and exited the track through the same opening left by Pagan's crash. Gray was not injured.

Jack Smith, one of the contenders for victory, also exited the track later in the race, bouncing over the guardrail. Actually, Smith's incident was the fourth of the day. One-time rookie sensation Jesse James Taylor, seriously injured in an Atlanta race several years earlier, had bounced atop the guardrail early in the race during his comeback attempt at Darlington. Neither Smith nor Taylor were injured, but as Jack Smith recalls, "Something like that got everybody's attention. It just proved what everybody was saying all along: That old track can jump up and bite you when you least expect it."

Undaunted by everything that happened, Fireball Roberts continued to run the high groove against the rail and went on to capture this spectacular Southern 500 by more than five laps over runner-up Buck Baker. Both drivers were in Chevrolets, and Roberts' pace was good enough to set a new record for the 500-mile distance at 102.48 mph.

How did drivers collect their winnings at Darlington in the early days? They waited at the payoff window. This photo includes Larry Frank (dressed in all white), Fireball Roberts, Herb Thomas, Jim Paschal and Tim Flock.

It took Roberts just four hours, 52 minutes and 44 seconds to complete the event, making it the first to be completed in less than five hours.

"Shorty" Rollins was third in a Ford, Jimmy Thompson followed in a Chevy and Marvin Panch was fifth in a Ford. Behind them, in order, were Convertible champion Bob Welborn, future NASCAR champion Rex White, Doug Cox, Bob Duell and Herb Estes.

Other notables in the 1958 Southern 500 included Junior Johnson (11th), Speedy Thompson (14th), Parnelli Jones (18th), Lee Petty (19th), Gene White (20th), Jim Paschal (21st) and Darlington rookie Herman (The Turtle) Beam (22nd), all finishing ahead of hotshoes Joe Weatherly (29th), Curtis Turner (33rd), Larry Frank (39th) and Cotton Owens (43rd).

The 1958 running of the Southern 500 would be the last time Darlington's Labor Day weekend would hold the distinction of being the only superspeedway 500-mile race on the NASCAR schedule. In February 1959, Daytona International Speedway and the Daytona 500 were born.

The Record Club & Hall of Fame

Bob Colvin, Darlington Raceway's president, was always thinking of ways to increase the national notoriety of this track.

One idea Colvin came up with was an exclusive club of Darlington drivers, which would consist of those who were fastest in qualifying for the Southern 500 in each different make of automobile, such as Chevrolet, Ford, Pontiac, Oldsmobile, Dodge, etc.

Colvin threw this idea out on the table during a meeting with Hale Talbert, vice-president of the Pure Oil Company, and Dick Dolan, Pure Oil's advertising manager. Pure Oil had mentioned to Colvin in 1959 that the company would be interested in doing something special for the drivers. As Dolan recalls, "We wanted to add some punch to Pure Oil's marketing program in racing."

So, in 1960, the Pure-Darlington Record Club was born, with Colvin and Dolan beating the drums. (Dolan would continue to beat the drums for his company and the Record Club for more than 30 years until he retired in Sun City, South Carolina, after the 1996 season.)

Membership in the Pure-Darlington Record Club would be awarded annually as a result of the previous year's qualifying results for the Southern 500. In addi-

(Above) Pure's Dick Dolan (left), who helped create the Pure Darlington Record Club in 1959, stands alongside NASCAR's John Bruner Sr., Fred Lorenzen, Darel Dieringer, Pure's J.C. Bradford, Darlington Raceway's Russ Catlin, Pure's Art Hammerstrom and Bob Colvin.

(Right) Dizzy Dean had a ball as guest speaker at the Pure Darlington Record Club dinner and shared a laugh with Darlington Police Chief J.C. Privette, who started the Southern 500 Parade.

Here's the first class of the Pure Darlington Record Club. Eight members were inducted as a result of the 1959 Southern 500 qualifying. The drivers were the quickest in their particular make of car. They included (l to r) Elmo Langley (Buick), Dick Joslin (Dodge), Marvin Panch (Ford), Speedy Thompson (Chevrolet), Joe Caspolich (Oldsmobile), Richard Petty (Plymouth) and Fireball Roberts (Pontiac). They were joined by Pure's Dick Dolan and the Raceway's Bob Colvin, who both initiated the formation of the club. Absent when this picture was taken was Bob Burdick, who qualified for the club in a Thunderbird. Fords and Thunderbirds were considered different makes, so Burdick had the fastest speed for a Thunderbird and Panch had the fastest Ford.

tion to membership, the club would offer its services in the form of a committee to instruct and approve rookie drivers for the Southern 500 (in cooperation with NASCAR).

Colvin and Dolan appropriately called it "The Most Exclusive Club in Motorsports," a tag that still holds true even though there are many more special programs designed for today's drivers and crews. The Pure-Darlington Record Club was the first, just like Darlington's Southern 500 was the first 500-mile race for stock car cars.

A blue dinner jacket was, and still is, given to members upon induction. If the new inductee is the fastest qualifier, he receives a white dinner jacket, emblematic of being the fastest overall, and a track record holder. In addition to the blazer, which makes them a member of an elite Darlington racing tradition, drivers also receive a special ring, a plaque, a driving uniform and prize money.

In 1960, the inaugural year, the fastest driver in each make of car received a $100 bonus, with the fastest driver overall receiving an additional $100. For stock car racing in those days, believe it or not, that kind of money was considered big bucks.

Eight drivers became charter members as a result of time trials for the Southern 500 in 1959. Pole-sitter Fireball Roberts, who was named the first president of the club, had the fastest Pontiac at 123.734 mph. Joe Caspolich (Olds), Elmo Langley (Buick), Marvin Panch (Ford), Richard Petty (Plymouth), Speedy Thompson (Chevrolet), Dick Joslin (Dodge) and Bob Burdick (Ford Thunderbird) completed the historic first group of inductees.

Another highlight for club members was an awards dinner with nationally-known, or, in some cases internationally-known, speakers and entertainers. The list of guests includes baseball great "Dizzy" Dean, world champion boxer Mickey Walker, Heisman Trophy winner and Green Bay

Packers star Paul Hornung, UCLA basketball legend John Wooden, Dallas Cowboys star and former University of South Carolina great Dan Reeves, pioneer golfer "Slammin' Sammy" Snead and many, many more.

The club is still going strong today. While the name has changed (it's now called the Union 76/Darlington Record Club), membership is still exclusive. Since the club began, 72 drivers have earned membership, including Fred Lorenzen, Darrell Waltrip, Junior Johnson, Cotton Owens and Cale Yarborough. Recently, such stars as Jeff Gordon, Dale Jarrett and John Andretti have proudly become members.

What makes the club so unique is its makeup. Of the 72 members, 19 are Hall of Famers, and only 18 have never won a NASCAR Winston Cup Series race. Nonetheless, they are considered equals by their peers when it comes to qualifying for the Southern 500 at Darlington. As Hall of Fame member Buddy Baker puts it, "Anybody that qualifies at Darlington ought to receive the Congressional Medal of Honor. Believe me, it takes hero-like courage to keep your foot on the gas during qualifying at the track 'Too Tough To Tame.'"

While they entered the Record Club as charter members, Joslin and Caspolich never won a NASCAR Winston Cup Series race. Neither did T.C. Hunt (1962), Neil Castles (1964), G.C. Spencer (1964), H.B. Bailey (1967), Walter Ballard (1972) and Earl Canavan (1979).

"That's really what makes the Union 76/Darlington Record Club so unique," says Dolan. "It's a special club for the guys who have had that quick moment of glory at Darlington. Even though they might not make a trip to victory lane, the Record Club is their victory lane. Membership is an honor and a treasure to some."

One of those was former driver and NASCAR official Elmo Langley, a charter member. "I wouldn't take anything for being a member," said Langley at the annual dinner one year. "All the old drivers share stories with the new drivers, and that makes it really unique in today's fast-paced environment. One thing has remained constant all those years: the track. Drivers and drivers' styles might have changed over the years, but Darlington hasn't changed."

Benny Parsons, a former NASCAR champion and popular television commentator today, puts it in perspective when he says, "To me, and to many other drivers, a big measure of becoming a real racer, is gaining membership in the Union 76/Darlington Record Club. It's not as easy as it might sound."

Actually, with a few minor changes, the rules are the same as they were in the beginning, over 40 years ago.

Dolan would be the first to tell you, no matter the name of the company (Pure Oil eventually underwent a succession of names, including Unocal, Union Oil of California,

UCLA Head Basketball Coach John Wooden was a guest speaker of the Pure Darlington Record Club in 1969. Sitting at the head table were (from left) H. B. Bailey, LeeRoy Yarbrough, Cale Yarborough, Pure's Bill McConnor, Darlington Raceway President Barney Wallace, Charlie Glotzbach and Darel Dieringer.

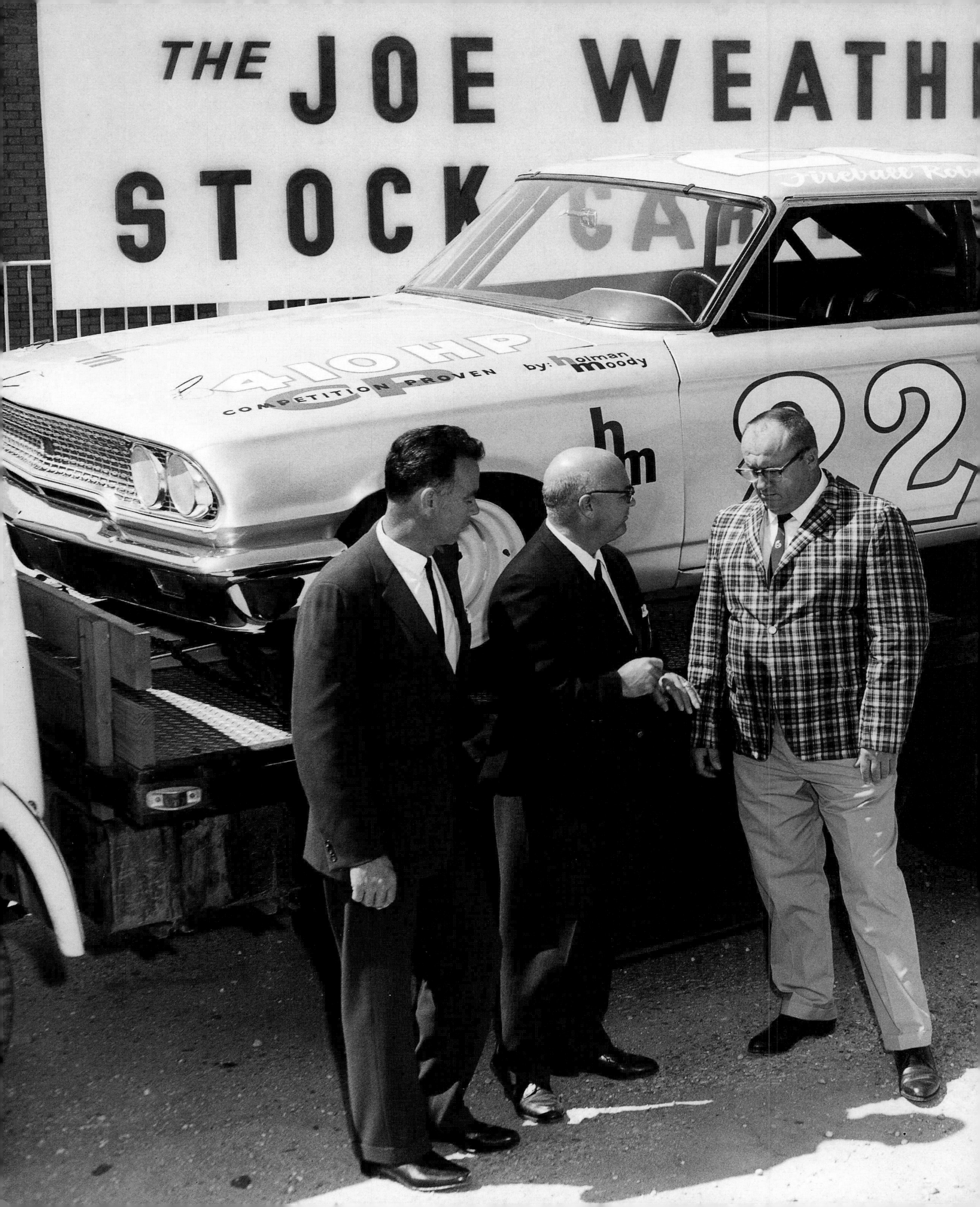

THE JOE
STOCK
410 HP
COMPETITION PROVEN
by: holman moody
hm
22

When the NMPA Stock Car Hall of Fame/Joe Weatherly Museum opened in 1965, car owners Ralph Moody (left) and John Holman (right) presented the museum and Raceway President Bob Colvin with Fireball Roberts' Ford.

Union 76 and, most recently, the Tosco Marketing Company.), his company was destined to maintain a presence in the sport overall, and a solid presence at Darlington Raceway in particular.

That Darlington presence included an exhibit for the Union 76/Darlington Record Club in the National Motorsports Press Association Stock Car Hall of Fame Museum (originally named the Joe Weatherly Stock Car Museum), when it opened in 1965. The museum was another brainchild of Bob Colvin.

The museum might have been Colvin's proudest accomplishment, named after Colvin's good friend and two-time NASCAR Champion Joe Weatherly, the "Clown Prince of Stock Car Racing," as journalist Bob Talbert so dubbed him.

Both Colvin and Weatherly liked practical jokes and played them on each other. Weatherly's most famous practical joke was his "mongoose in a cage" routine. He had a foxtail nailed inside a small cage and had a sign on the outside that read, "Danger, Mongoose Inside!" When folks leaned over to take a closer look, Weatherly would trigger a hatch and the foxtail would pop out into the face of the terrified onlooker.

While Weatherly made many the brunt of his jokes, Colvin had the last laugh on one occasion. Colvin made a wager with Weatherly, and if Weatherly lost, he agreed to ride a donkey in the Southern 500 parade. True to his word, and much to the delight of Colvin and the parade watchers, Weatherly wound up on the back of a burro.

To Darlington, Weatherly was more than a race driver, more than a happy little man wearing black-and-white saddle shoes. The Virginia native was an integral part of Darlington's early success.

The pair of southern characters went to Indianapolis a few years before Weatherly's death at Riverside in 1964, and Little Joe, after watching the Indianapolis cars for the first time and touring the Indianapolis Motor Speedway Museum, told Colvin he ought to build a museum for stock cars at Darlington. "These things look like cucumbers with hayraker wheels," said Weatherly in reference to the Indy cars. "They don't even have fenders."

Following Weatherly's death, Colvin brought plans for the Joe Weatherly Stock Car Museum before Darlington Raceway's Board of Directors. Jack Tyler of Florence, S.C., drew up the plans and the Raceway unanimously approved them. The Museum was officially dedicated on May 2, 1965. South Carolina Senator Strom Thurmond, who, as Governor, cut the ribbon in pre-race ceremonies during the 1950 event, dedicated the Museum in similar fashion during formal opening ceremonies.

Four Hall of Famers were inducted in 1965, the first

National Motorsports Press Association President Benny Phillips presented NASCAR founder Bill France Sr., with his plaque after France was inducted into the NMPA Stock Car Hall of Fame in 1975.

year, including legendary mechanic Paul McDuffie, who set up cars driven by Fireball Roberts, Joe Lee Johnson and Bob Welborn. Fireball Roberts, winner of 32 races during his 15-year career, was also inducted, along with Herb Thomas, who won two NASCAR championships as well as three Southern 500's. Weatherly, for whom the Museum was named, was also inducted the first year.

Each year, members of the press association vote for new Hall of Fame inductees, much in the same fashion as other sports do. Induction ceremonies are held each year during festivities leading up to the Southern 500. Each Hall of Fame member is showcased in the Museum with a pylon featuring an artist's rendering of the member, various memorabilia from that member's racing career and an audio description by popular motorsports announcer Eli Gold.

The NMPA/Joe Weatherly Stock Car Museum Hall of Fame is a storehouse of stock car racing treasures. A total of 15 historic cars are on display in the museum, including Johnny Mantz's Plymouth (winner of the first Southern 500 in 1950) and Herb Thomas' Hudson Hornet (winner of the 1951 Southern 500).

Two convertibles, Curtis Turner's 1956 Ford and Bob Welborn's 1957 Chevrolet, are also part of the exhibits. Other winning cars include Jim Reed's 1959 Chevrolet (the first car to win Darlington on Goodyear tires); Junior Johnson's 1963 Chevrolet, winner of seven races during the 1963 season; Fireball Roberts' 1963 Ford he drove to his second Southern 500 win; Fred Lorenzen's 1966 Ford that carried "Fearless Freddie" to his outstanding $100,000 season, the first time in history a driver won more than $100,000; Richard Petty's 1967 Plymouth that won a record 23 races that year; Buddy Baker's 1969 Dodge Charger, winner of the Southern 500 in 1970; David Pearson's famed 1971 Mercury, which claimed 11 victories in 18 starts during the 1973 season; Cale Yarborough's 1980 Oldsmobile, winner of six races; Bill Elliott's 1985 Ford Thunderbird, which won the historic Winston Million with a Southern 500 victory that earned the Dawsonville, Ga., native the nickname, "Million Dollar Bill;" Joe Weatherly's 1964 Mercury prepared by veteran chief mechanic Bud Moore; and the remnants of Darrell Waltrip's mangled Chevrolet that rolled down the Daytona backstretch too many times to count.

Today, there are 55 members of the NMPA Hall of Fame. The latest inductee (1998) was none other than "The King," Richard Petty, whose record speaks for itself.

With Colvin running the ship, the Raceway made many strides during its early years. He elevated the stature of the race by promoting "pomp and circumstance" surrounding Darlington's events, the Southern 500 in particular. He helped create the Miss Southern 500 Beauty Pageant along with the city of Darlington Police Department, and he created the Southern 500 Parade with the help of the

Former Lightweight boxing champ Mickey Walker has a laugh with Buddy Baker during the 1964 Pure Darlington Record Club dinner.

(From left) T.C. Hunt, Curtis "Crawfish" Crider, Glenn "Fireball" Roberts, Richard Petty, Fred Lorenzen and Buck Baker pose for a picture at the Pure Darlington Record Club dinner.

prestolite

Pontiac conducted a 24-hour endurance run and set a record at Darlington. Drivers participating included (l-r) Indy driver Len Sutton, Joe Weatherly (NASCAR), Indy winner Roger Ward, Fireball Roberts (NASCAR), Marvin Panch (NASCAR) and Paul Goldsmith (NASCAR & Indy).

The Pure Record Club has always been a part of the NMPA Stock Car Hall of Fame/Joe Weatherly Museum.

Darlington Jaycees. He dreamed up a Johnny Reb character symbolizing his beloved South, waving a giant Confederate Flag and riding the hoods of winning cars into victory lane.

Colvin also brought in a knowledgeable press agent, Russ Catlin, a veteran of Indianapolis 500 activities. Together, the two of them lived by the credo, "It doesn't matter what the newspapers say about you, as long as they spell your name right." With Colvin the willing pitchman, Catlin staged press conferences up and down the East Coast touting Darlington's Southern 500 festivities as the "biggest spectacle in stock car racing!"

It was Colvin's idea to spruce up the Southern 500 Parade and Miss Southern 500 Beauty Pageant with visiting celebrities serving as Grand Marshals, the first of whom was universally-popular James Arness, better-known as Matt Dillon, star of the television series "Gunsmoke."

Dillon's presence at the 1958 Southern 500 gave the event added stature – Hollywood-type stature – with folks saying, "Hey, this has got to be a pretty big event if Matt

(Above) Buck Baker (#47) duels with his son Buddy Baker (#87) during the 1960 Southern 500. This time around, father came out on top, capturing his second of three Labor Day triumphs. Notice the old guardrail, which lined the corners. NMPA Hall of Famer Jack Smith owned Buck's Pontiac.

(Left) In 1960, the Rebel 300 for NASCAR's Convertible Division was halted on lap 74 for inclement weather and had to be finished a week later. Joe Weatherly (center) won the race. Prior to the restart, Larry Frank (Gabriel shirt, clockwise), Banjo Matthews, Fireball Roberts, Weatherly, John Holman (pointing), Herb Nab and Bobby Johns engage in some pit road politicking.

Dillon wants to attend it." Dillon was seen everywhere – in the parade, at the beauty pageant and riding around the track in the pace car before the race.

By the time the 1959 Rebel 300 rolled around, Darlington Raceway was presenting the second superspeedway race of the year. Big Bill France had succeeded in building the mammoth, two-and-a-half-mile Daytona International Speedway in Daytona Beach, Fla.

The Rebel 300 for NASCAR Convertibles on Saturday, May 9, was won by Fireball Roberts in a Chevrolet. Roberts beat Joe Weatherly to the finish line by almost a lap. Larry Frank was third, Bob Burdick fourth and Rex White fifth. The race was the first in Darlington history to be completed without a caution flag.

This race also marked the end of what was known as NASCAR's "strictly" convertible division at Darlington. However, promoters Colvin and Bill France, the head of NASCAR, figured out a way to keep the convertibles rolling at Darlington.

Colvin and France decided the spring Darlington event would remain just for the ragtops. So, from 1960 through 1962, convertibles continued to maneuver their way around one track, and one track only – Darlington, in the Rebel 300.

The 1960 edition of the Rebel 300 was one in which Colvin got directly involved. The race started on Saturday, May 7, but on lap 58, rain began to fall. The race was stopped on lap 74 with Roberts in the lead, and was to be

Marshall Matt Dillon (James Arness) meets one of NASCAR's finest, Curtis Turner.

Here's three tough guys at the track Too Tough To Tame – former lightweight boxing champion Willie Pep, Paul Goldsmith and Curtis Turner.

resumed one week later. Controversy followed.

NASCAR first said the cars would be impounded, but could be serviced before the race restarted, which would be under the green flag. Protests came about because some drivers had taken advantage of the caution for rain the week before to refuel, and were ready to go. So NASCAR reversed the ruling, saying the race would restart under caution.

Weatherly, who had pitted under caution the week earlier, wasn't his normal joking self with this particular situation. He went on the offensive, appearing on radio and television programs stating his case for a green-flag restart. A 24-hour police guard was brought in during the week. More than 10,000 additional fans showed up a week later in response to all the controversy, with an abundance of yellow and green flags filling the stands.

Colvin, of course, sided with his longtime friend, Weatherly. He could also play a part in the restart since he was the driver of the pace car. Colvin stirred the pot all week, saying the pace laps "would be the fastest in history." And they were.

All the green-yellow controversy ended when Roberts had mechanical problems and fell out of the race. Weatherly took over and led the final 46 laps. Richard Petty was second, followed by Rex White, Lee Petty and Buck Baker.

Weeks later, Colvin was

(Above) Ever hear of the slogan "Ram Tough?" Well, 1966 Southern 500 winner Darel Dieringer and car owner Bob Osiecki pose with their personal goat in front of their "Ram Tough" Dodge convertible in the Darlington garage.

(Right) An All American trio – Junior Johnson (left), Ned Jarrett and Bob Colvin (right).

still feeling some heat from fans about his role in the affair. Driving the pace car through another state one day, he was stopped by a law officer. "You were doing 90 mph in a 30 mph zone," said the officer.

Colvin protested. The policeman knew Colvin. "This is the Darlington pace car and you drove it 90 mph when you should have run 30 mph! You cost Fireball the race and me $25 bucks that I had bet on him. So, you can either post a $25 bond or go to jail!"

Colvin paid, grinning all the while. "Hell, I'd a been mad, too, if I had lost $25.00!"

Another unusual incident occurred in that same 1960 event. Driver Johnny Allen, from Spartanburg, S.C., took a wild, bizarre ride over the guardrail in the fourth turn on

lap 148 and slammed into the scoring stand, sending one-third of the structure to its knees. Luckily, no one was injured.

"I think there were a few of us who had to go change our underwear," joked Morris Metcalfe, NASCAR's Chief Scorer and Timer who was in the scoring stand that day. "It scared us and some of us were a little shaken."

NASCAR red-flagged the race to get the scorers down and in another position for the rest of the event.

"The problem was we couldn't get down," added Metcalfe. "Allen's car knocked down the steps and we were stuck 50 feet in the air. They brought a fire truck and placed it on the race track and raised the ladder to where we were.

"We all got on our hands and knees, one at a time, and inched our way across the ladder, having to look straight down. Some may have been shaken, but we had to finish scoring the race, and that's what we did.

"I've scored nearly 3,200 races in my lifetime," says Metcalfe, "and I never saw anything like that day at Darlington. I'll never forget it."

Jack Smith of Greenville, S.C., was one who was biting his nails in the late stages of the 1960 Southern 500. A Hall of Famer today, Smith had gone completely out of the track two years earlier in turn one.

"We were running second to Fireball in 1958 and my car decided it wanted to go to the right instead of the left," said

Jim Paschal shows how helmets have changed over the years.

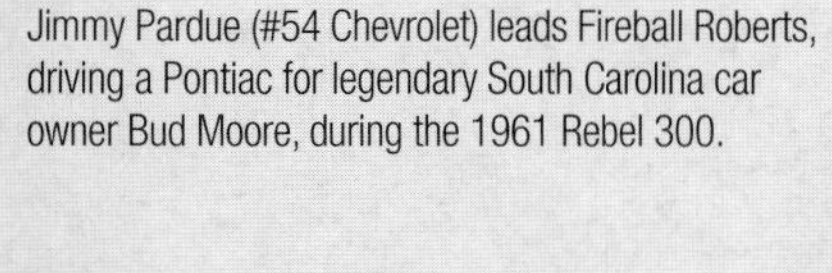

Jimmy Pardue (#54 Chevrolet) leads Fireball Roberts, driving a Pontiac for legendary South Carolina car owner Bud Moore, during the 1961 Rebel 300.

Smith. "Jim Reed dropped an engine right in front of me and I hit his oil. I went over the rail, and every time it hit, it hit the nose or the trunk lid. You had never seen a car so torn up. The only thing I saved from it was the roll bars. The rest went to the junkyard. I got to where I didn't want to race Darlington. I'd sometimes qualify the car then put someone else in it. It wasn't that I still couldn't get around the place well; I just knew others could get around it better than me."

He let Buck Baker handle the driving chores in 1960, and Baker didn't disappoint car owner Smith. In a three-driver duel to the finish, Baker led Fireball Roberts and Richard Petty. With 11 laps to go, Roberts' engine soured, and with three circuits remaining, Petty blew a tire. Baker found himself all alone on the lead lap.

But, with a lap and one-half to go, Baker popped a tire. He spun the Pontiac, but gained control and limped home on the apron of the track, just ahead of Rex White.

"I hit both the outside wall and inside wall when the tire blew," said Baker. "There I was sitting all by myself with a flat tire watching the field move by, and I couldn't get the car started. The gears, all except fourth, were jammed because of the impact. Finally, I slipped the clutch and got moving again.

"At the end, I pulled into the garage. I thought Rex had won. I thought he had made up three laps on me while I

These squeaky-clean convertibles of Joe Weatherly and Curtis Turner get checked under the hood in the garage area. The Convertibles ran at Darlington from 1957 through 1962. Both Turner (1958) and Weatherly (1960) drove ragtops to victory at Darlington.

Fred Lorenzen, sporting his unique Rebel 300 Darlington shirt, is all smiles after winning the 1961 Rebel 300. Joining in the celebration is crew chief Herb Nab (left), Miss Southern 500 Mary Ann Brunnerman and car owner Ralph Moody.

was limping to the finish line, but then they announced I had won."

Jim Paschal was third, Emanuel Zervakis fourth and Ned Jarrett fifth. Roberts, who won the pole, was ninth after breaking an axle late in the event.

Incidentally, a young driver by the name of David Pearson, from Spartanburg, S.C., started 22nd in his initial outing at Darlington in 1960. He suffered a broken axle and finish 27th, but Pearson was destined to become Darlington's all-time NASCAR Winston Cup Series win leader, despite his unimpressive debut.

The following year was the first time all the cars were hauled to the track. Drivers could no longer drive the family sedan to the track, taping up the headlights and strapping the doors shut. Some drivers also began to sport custom-made uniforms.

The 1961 Rebel 300 helped to create a new superstar in NASCAR – a real media darling. His name was Fred Lorenzen, from Elmhurst, Ill. Driving for the Holman-Moody factory Ford team, he came to Darlington hoping to make his mark.

A host of drivers took turns at the lead, but when it counted, the event came down to a trio – the new kid on the block, Lorenzen, along with veterans Fireball Roberts and Curtis Turner. Roberts was seeking his third Rebel 300 win, and Turner, "Ol' Leadfoot" as he was called, would press the gas pedal through the floor. When it came to NASCAR's original superspeedway, Curtis Turner always said, "Little boys don't race at Darlington."

Lorenzen made his way to the front with a car that handled perfectly in the turns, while Roberts was superfast on the straights. Late in the

On Your Mark! Get Set! Go! Fred Lorenzen and Fireball Roberts, who occupied the front row, are set for the start of the 1961 Rebel 300.

race, Roberts and Lorenzen fell victim to pit stops. Enter Turner, the old pro who inherited the lead with 20 laps to go. Trailing in a distant second, Lorenzen would make a charge like no one had ever seen.

Slowly, he whittled away at the lead. Catching Turner was one thing; passing him was another. No one witnessing the race gave Lorenzen a chance. Turner was the old master, who knew every trick to stay in front. Everyone remembered the 1958 Darlington duel, when Turner gave Weatherly a love tap and went on to win. Turner didn't give anyone an inch.

Lorenzen caught Turner, and the fender banging began. Lap after lap, with the crowd on its feet, the two cars touched. Then, with less than two laps to go, Turner drifted high and Lorenzen dove low. Lorenzen pushed past Turner in the first turn, sliding all the way to the guardrail. The race was "Fearless Freddie's" the rest of the way.

"We must have bumped each other 50 times in those final 20 laps," Lorenzen said. "I had a lot of momentum built up on him coming off turn four, so I decided to fake him on the outside and go underneath him. That's what I did. It was the biggest win of my life."

(Right) Miss Southern 500 Mary Ann Brunnerman presents the 1962 Rebel 300 winner's trophy to Nelson Stacy as Hall of Fame car owner Ralph Moody (left) looks on.

(Below) In his first attempt, Nelson Stacy won the 1961 Southern 500.

Lorenzen averaged 110.520 mph and won by six car-lengths. Johnny Allen was third, followed by Burdick and Roberts.

After his 1961 Rebel win, Lorenzen was one of the favorites for the Labor Day Southern 500. He qualified second behind his idol, Roberts, who claimed his sixth career pole at Darlington. The man they both had to worry about, however, was starting third – an unheralded driver out of Cincinnati, Ohio, named Nelson Stacy from the USAC ranks.

"Before the race, they gave me a hard time, said I was

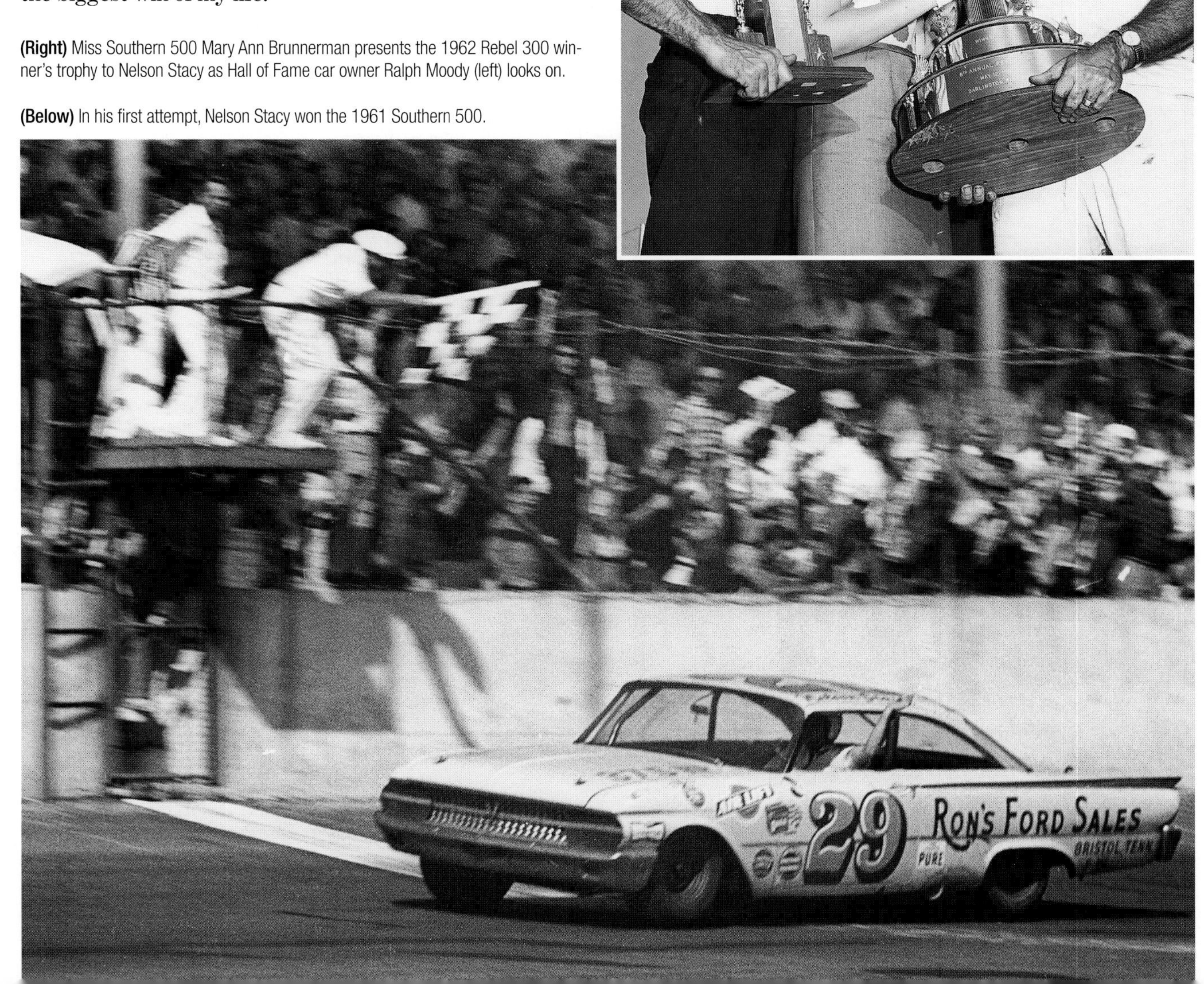

(Above) Hall of Famer Junior Johnson listens to Bob Colvin, former President of Darlington.

(Right) Although he wasn't flagged the winner, Larry Frank, from Spartanburg, S.C., captured the 1962 Southern 500. After a scoring recheck the night after the race, the win was taken away from Junior and awarded to Frank the next day.

unheard of, that I lacked experience," said Stacy, who earlier in the year, competed for the first time at Darlington in the Rebel 300, finishing 11th.

While the media may not have known who he was, the fans always love an underdog, which is exactly what Stacy was. This was his first attempt in NASCAR's Grand Ol' Race, and he intended to make a statement.

After Roberts and Lorenzen swapped the lead back and forth, Stacy vaulted to the point on lap 113 of the 364-lap event. When Lorenzen exited the race on lap 158 with a throttle problem, it became a two-horse race between Stacy and Roberts, the seasoned veteran.

With 87 laps to go, however, Roberts dove into the pits and jumped out of his car with neck cramps. In crawled Marvin Panch, another veteran who knew his way around Darlington. Panch held a comfortable lead with 30 laps remaining, but a caution came out and allowed Stacy to pull up to his rear bumper.

Stacy made his move down the frontstretch and passed Panch down low into turn one with six laps remaining. He went on to

(Above) A driver knew he was getting everything out of his car when he received his "Darlington Stripe," a scrape with the fourth-turn guardrail. Here, Ned Jarrett checks out his right-rear quarter panel after making contact with the rail in 1963. Two years later, Jarrett won the 1965 Southern 500.

(Right) Ah, the familiar smile of a young Richard Petty. He won three times at Darlington, all coming in 1966-67.

win by 2.64 seconds in his Holman-Moody Ford to become the only rookie besides Johnny Mantz – winner of the first Southern 500 – to win the classic. A lap back in third was David Pearson, with Jim Paschal fourth and Emanuel Zervakis fifth. A new name on the horizon, Cale Yarborough, made his first Darlington start and finished 30th with a blown engine.

Stacy felt like he had mastered Darlington and knew his way around the track, knowing all about the so-called "Darlington Stripe." He said the third and fourth turns were the keys to the track, describing the entrance to the third turn as "One-Way Alley."

"It's possible to wear a hole in the side of your car during a race," Stacy said. "You're going to hit that rail a lot in a 500-mile race. You're back in that same place every 38 seconds. I love it."

In the 1962 Rebel race, Stacy set out to prove that his triumph was no fluke. Again, the victim was Panch, who was driving the Wood Brothers Ford. This was a special event, being the final Convertible race ever staged.

In his attempt to make it three straight, Stacy finished seventh in the 1962 Southern 500 after being lapped by Junior Johnson early in the race. Johnson, who started on the outside of the front row alongside Fireball Roberts, was flagged the winner with Marvin Panch second, David Pearson third, ex-Marine Larry Frank fourth, Jim Paschal fifth and Richard Petty sixth.

Johnson went to victory lane. Frank, meanwhile, figured he had won the race. Near midnight, after a recheck of all the scoring cards, NASCAR Chief Scorer Joe Epton made an official statement that Frank's scorer had missed a lap that Frank had completed. He, indeed, had won the race, leading the final 85 laps. The next day, Frank, an independent, was presented the trophy in front of empty grandstands. Johnson was relegated to second, with Panch third, Pearson fourth, Petty fifth and Paschal sixth.

Since its inception, the 300-miler had been run by Convertibles, but with 1962 as the final event for ragtops staged at the historical facility, the 1963 Rebel 300 would be a product of Colvin's imagination. Colvin decided to use a new twist and run a Monza-style split race. "We'll use one of those 'Lee-Manz (LeMans)' starts off the grid," Colvin said with a grin. "That oughta be something." And, it was.

The plan, copied from that which had worked so successfully in Monza, Italy, included a running start and a standing start for two 150-mile races. A 30-minute compulsory pit stop between the two sprint races would give teams some time to adjust their cars for the second race. Based on a special point system for the event, the combined finishes of the two races determined the overall winner, making it possible for a driver to win the event without leading a lap.

Fred Lorenzen started from the pole in his Holman-Moody Ford and was flanked by Tiny Lund in the Wood Brothers Ford. The start resembled a battle royal. The front-row drivers slammed hard into each other, and Lorenzen slipped back only to tangle with Rex White. The duo crashed and only completed two laps.

At the end of the first segment, Joe Weatherly, driving a Pontiac for South Carolina's Bud Moore, zoomed past Junior Johnson on the final lap to win. Third went to Fireball Roberts.

In the second segment, the checkered flag fell on Richard Petty, but it was Weatherly who went to the winner's circle. His second-place run behind Petty in the second part of the race gave him the most overall points. Roberts, who finished third in both events in his Ford,

(Left) In the unique two-part Rebel 300 in 1963, Joe Weatherly (center) gave South Carolina's Bud Moore (right) his first Darlington victory as a car owner. That's Miss Southern 500, Joyce Brown, on the left.

(Right) It was a hot day for Weatherly at Darlington during this race in the 1960s. After falling out early, he was found on pit road with his shoes off, soothing his feet with water. Notice his shoes to his right, and also take note of his fingerless gloves.

REBEL
300
26
REBEL "300"
SOUTHERN
DARLINGTON, S.C.
STOP WATCH
87

Two-time NASCAR Winston Cup Series Champion Ned Jarrett's proudest moment came when he won the 1965 Southern 500 at Darlington. That's a young James Hylton, who later became a driver, helping pit the Bondy Long-owned Ford driven by Jarrett.

JOHN

Victory Lane was filled with excitement when Ned Jarrett won the 1965 Southern 500. Greeting him after the triumph were Bob Colvin (glasses), South Carolina Governor Bob McNair and actor Ken Curtis, otherwise known as Festus on the television hit "Gunsmoke."

took second overall, and Petty, sixth in the opener and the winner of the second race, was third overall. Lund was fourth and Bobby Johns fifth.

Weatherly went on to win the NASCAR Grand National Championship in 1963. He died at Riverside the following January.

Although Lorenzen suffered bad luck in the 1963 Rebel 300, he was a man on a mission. In the end, he would finish the 1963 season third in points and become the first driver in history to win over $100,000 ($122,578.28) in a single season.

With General Motors officially out of the sport (although Junior Johnson's Ray Fox-prepared Chevy was the hottest car on the track most of the year), the 1963 Southern 500 was primarily a Ford battleground, with Fred Lorenzen and Fireball Roberts leading the charge.

Roberts shot past Lorenzen on lap 332 of the 364-lap race and sped to a 17-second victory in his Holman-Moody Ford. He averaged a record 129.784 mph, easily besting the old mark of 117.960 mph set a year earlier by Larry Frank. The first four finishers were Fords with Marvin Panch second, Lorenzen third and Nelson Stacy fourth. Darel Dieringer, in a Mercury, was fifth.

Lorenzen won the Rebel 300 the next year, his second triumph in the spring 300-miler. Roberts was second and Junior Johnson third, followed by Ned Jarrett and Jimmy Pardue. All top-five finishers drove Fords.

Roberts' second-place run in the 1964 Rebel 300 would be his final appearance at Darlington. His Southern 500 victo-

Like they do today, drivers supported area charitable events in the 1960s. (From left) Buck Baker, Fred Lorenzen, Joe Weatherly and Fireball Roberts joined the U.S. Navy's Blue Angels for this charity bowling event.

ry the year before, his second in the Labor Day classic, was his 32nd career win. It would also be his final triumph. He died in July of 1964 as a result of burns he received in a fiery crash at Charlotte.

Four years after grabbing what he called his biggest win ever, the 1960 Southern 500, Buck Baker came to Darlington in a Ray Fox Dodge hoping to win his third Darlington classic. Baker also won in 1953.

Here's a young Cale Yarborough prior to the 1963 Southern 500. Yarborough started 21st and finished 17th. Today, he is the all-time winner of the Southern 500 with five triumphs.

While young lions Richard Petty, David Pearson, Junior Johnson and Jimmy Pardue raced to the front, old pro Baker used his experience and established a pace designed to put him in contention at the end of the race. Petty dominated for 252 laps, but had trouble and gave way to Baker, who would gain his 46th and final NASCAR career victory.

Jim Paschal was second in a Petty Plymouth, followed by Petty, who suffered ignition problems and lost time in the pits. Ned Jarrett was fourth in the Bondy Long Ford, with Pardue fifth in a Plymouth.

While Baker's Dodge won the 1964 Southern 500, it was hard to find a competitive Chrysler product at NASCAR events in 1965. In a conflict over rules, Chrysler and its drivers boycotted the 1965 NASCAR season. Richard Petty did some exhibition drag racing, as did David Pearson, who also joined Paul Goldsmith and Bobby Isaac in occasional USAC (United States Auto Club) stock car races in the Midwest.

Neil Castles and Bunkie Blackburn were the only Plymouth drivers in the field for the 1965 Rebel 300. For the fifth straight time, Fred Lorenzen was the fastest qualifier, but Junior Johnson dominated the race, leading 197 of the 219 laps.

On his final pit stop, Junior's Ford slipped past his pit stall. His crew ran to the car, serviced it and pushed it to get it started again. Johnson came out of the pits and passed Darel Dieringer with 12 laps to go. Dieringer's car owner, Bud Moore, filed a protest since NASCAR rules stated if a car goes past the assigned pit area, it has to make another lap and stop in the proper pit stall.

NASCAR ruled that Johnson did not violate the rules because the pit area past his stall was not being used. The victory stood, and Dieringer was listed second. Ned Jarrett finished third, Dick Hutcherson fourth and Bobby Johns fifth.

Jarrett had been getting closer and closer to a triumph at Darlington in his Bondy Long-owned Ford. Now living in nearby Camden (where car owner Long had a garage), Jarrett felt like Darlington was his hometown track. The Southern 500 was THE race he wanted to win.

The 1965 Southern 500 was a wreck-filled event that came down to a two-car battle between Fred Lorenzen and Darel Dieringer, while Jarrett paced himself. But Lorenzen blew an engine with less than 50 laps to go, and, at the

Fred Lorenzen, who won five straight pole positions (1961-65) for the Rebel 300, flashes past the start/finish line in his Holman-Moody Ford. Lorenzen won two Rebel 300s, in 1961 and 1964.

same moment, smoke began billowing from underneath Dieringer's Mercury. With 39 laps left, Jarrett slipped past Dieringer and went on to win by an incredible 14 laps over defending Southern 500 champion Buck Baker, who had relief help from his son Buddy.

Dieringer, who was 19 laps behind, still wound up third, followed by Roy Mayne and Buddy Arrington.

"I had already conceded that I could not win unless something happened to Fred and Darel," said Jarrett. "I backed off to about 117 mph in the final 20 laps to let the car cool off. At one point, I was afraid they might black flag me for going too slow."

The most spectacular wreck in the race occurred on lap 118 when Cale Yarborough tangled with Sam McQuagg and rocketed into the air over the turn one guardrail. His car flipped outside the track and came to rest against a light pole in a parking lot. Neither driver was hurt.

The race was also a tragic one. Buren Skeen suffered multiple internal injuries and a basal skull fracture after being broadsided by Reb Wickersham's Ford. Nine days later, Skeen died in a hospital.

Two weeks before the 1966 Rebel 300, Ford parked its cars and drivers in protest of NASCAR's rules. Fred Lorenzen, defending Southern 500 champion Ned Jarrett, Dick Hutcherson, who had finished fourth the year before and Marvin Panch were on the sidelines. Only 10 Fords entered the event, all of which were fielded by independents.

There was also a new element to the 1966 Rebel 300: It became the Rebel 400. And this race was Richard Petty's from the start. Petty totally dominated the event, leading 271 of 291 laps, including the final 190. At the end of 400 miles, he had a three-lap lead over second-place Paul Goldsmith (Plymouth), who had passed David Pearson (Dodge) after Pearson cracked a wheel in the latter part of the race. Bunkie Blackburn in a Dodge and G.C. Spencer in a Plymouth rounded out the top five. The top Ford was

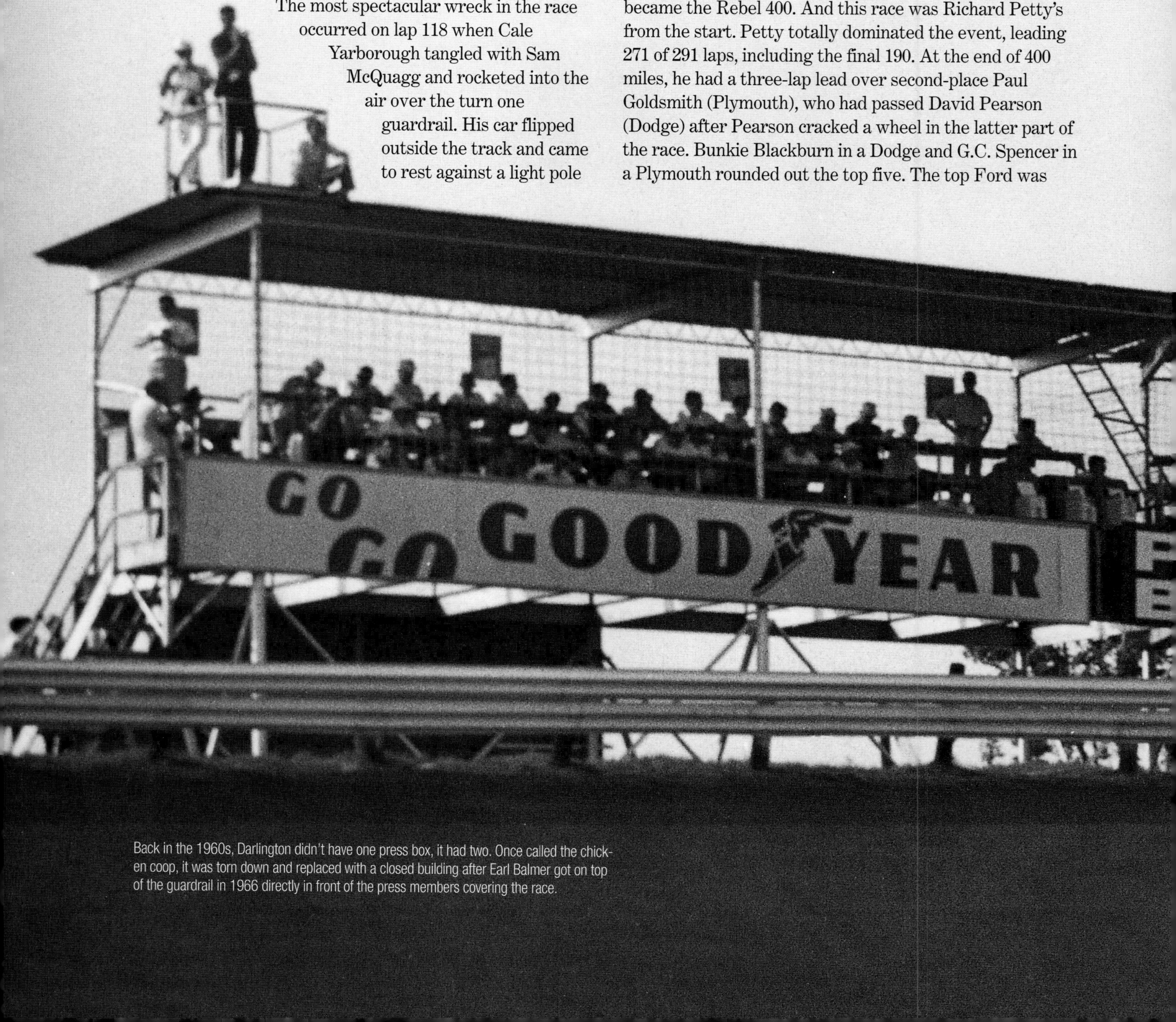

Back in the 1960s, Darlington didn't have one press box, it had two. Once called the chicken coop, it was torn down and replaced with a closed building after Earl Balmer got on top of the guardrail in 1966 directly in front of the press members covering the race.

Elmo Langley, who finished seventh.

"A Petty has finally won at Darlington," said Petty afterwards. "My father (Lee) ran here a bunch and could never get here (victory lane). I've been close so many times. Today was just our day!"

With the Rebel 400 win, Petty was even more anxious to win the Southern 500, NASCAR's original masterpiece. In the 1966 Southern 500, Petty and third-place starter Darel Dieringer, trying to give car owner Bud Moore his second win at Darlington, battled most of the day, swapping the lead back and forth. Petty led seven times; Dieringer led eight times.

In the homestretch, Petty appeared to be a shoe-in for victory, but a slow-leaking tire slowed him down and, seven laps from the end, Dieringer roared past. Petty hung on for second place. David Pearson was third, Marvin Panch fourth and Fred Lorenzen finished fifth.

Petty was involved in a bizarre incident on lap 189 when he went to lap Earl Balmer, who was four laps down. The two touched, and Balmer's Dodge went into the guardrail in the first turn. It then climbed on top of the guardrail and slid along the silver steel, sending debris and gas into the open press box, which sat just outside the turn.

It tore 100 feet of steel guardrail onto the track and destroyed eight fence posts. "I thought sure as hell I was going into the press box," said a shaken Balmer. "I don't know what happened. I didn't see Petty."

The media jokingly referred to the press box after that as "Balmer's Box." A new press box would be a challenge for the good-natured Colvin, who said he would build one in the near future. It was one of the few projects Colvin couldn't complete.

On January 24, 1967, Colvin died in his Raceway office of a massive heart attack at the age of 47.

Barney Wallace, an original board member, was named president before the 1967 Rebel 400.

Richard Petty had even more reason to win the springtime classic this time around. His next NASCAR triumph would give him his 55th career win, pushing him past his retired father, Lee, the all-time leader in NASCAR wins. Such a historic occasion should happen at Darlington, and it did.

Petty dominated once again to gain his second victory at Darlington in his last three attempts. He led a convincing 266 of a possible 291 laps and beat David Pearson to the finish line by a lap. It was Pearson's first ride with the Holman-Moody team.

All the years of bad luck that hounded Petty in the Southern 500 came to a crashing halt in 1967. Second-place starter Buddy Baker wrecked, third-place starter Cale Yarborough ran only three laps before he blew an engine. Defending champion Darel Dieringer bashed the front end of his car 15 minutes into the race and was never a factor.

Petty, in a Plymouth, won by five laps over David Pearson (Ford), who had relief help from Yarborough. G.C. Spencer was third in another Petty Plymouth, with "Chargin'" Charlie Glotzbach fourth and "Little Bud" Moore from Charleston, fifth. Rookie Donnie Allison finished in sixth place.

No South Carolina-born drivers had ever won at the "Granddaddy of Superspeedways," South Carolina's own Darlington Raceway. But times were changing, and two Palmetto State young guns were on the rise in 1968.

David Pearson, in his first full season with the Holman-Moody team, was looking to give his factory-backed squad their first triumph at Darlington in four years. Pearson, who would later be given the nickname the "Silver Fox," could have been called that after the 1968 Rebel 400 – or at least his team could have been called that.

Pearson was piloting a Ford with a 396 cubic-inch engine. According to NASCAR's cubic inch-to-weight ratio in 1968, Pearson's car was allowed to weigh 293 pounds less than cars with larger, more powerful motors. Pearson's thinking then, and now, was that you don't have to have just raw power to win at Darlington. Handling in the corners is the key, and the bigger-engine cars burn up rubber faster in the turns.

They were right. Pearson led 131 of the 291 laps and was 18 seconds ahead of Darel Dieringer when the checkered flag dropped. Pearson went on in 1968 to capture his first of two straight NASCAR championships for the Holman-Moody team. Coupled with his 1966 title while driving for

Big John Sears, Bobby Isaac and Paul Goldsmith take a timeout and relax on the pit rail at Darlington. Note the car in the background, a Plymouth Roadrunner.

(Above) Who was the first man to win the "Triple Crown?" It was none other than LeeRoy Yarbrough, who pulled off the feat after winning the 1969 Southern 500 at Darlington. David Pearson did it again, in 1976, and in 1985, Winston gave $1 million to a driver who could win three of the big four races. Bill Elliott captured the bonus with his win in the 1985 Southern 500 at Darlington. Jeff Gordon matched Elliott in 1997.

(Right) In their younger days ... Current Darlington Raceway President Jim Hunter shares a laugh with Richard Petty in Darlington's garage area.

Cotton Owens, Pearson won the championship three times – the only times he ran the full circuit.

Cale Yarborough might have been remembered for his flight over the first-turn guardrail in 1965 while battling with Sam McQuagg, but the South Carolina native's biggest win, and the one he recalls today as his finest hour, was the 1968 Southern 500.

Yarborough gave the Wood Brothers their first victory at Darlington, leading five times for 175 laps. It was the final 50 laps, however, that told the tale.

The cars were quicker than ever, averaging just a shade less than 150 mph. The track had basically one groove and passing was difficult. If a driver could get in front and hold his line, he could win. The situation fit Yarborough to a tee.

The faster Pearson, chasing his first Southern 500 win, hounded Yarborough, glued to his back bumper. Heading into turn one, Pearson dove underneath Yarborough and the two cars collided. Pearson looped his car in the infield while Yarborough bounced off the guardrail and continued. Pearson couldn't make up the lost ground and finished second.

"It was the first big track and the first one I knew any-

thing about," said a jubilant Yarborough after the race. "I hung on the fence as a spectator, climbed under the fence, then got thrown out of the place when I was 16 years old for trying to race. Nobody will ever know how much winning the Southern 500 means to me."

This was also the last race on the "old" Darlington. After the race, turns three and four were reworked to their current 25-degree banking to make a wider racing groove, and the track received a completely new asphalt surface.

While a Cale Yarborough won the last Southern 500 on the old Darlington, a driver by the name of LeeRoy Yarbrough (no relation, different name) would conclude the 1960s at Darlington with two victories.

Yarbrough, in a three-car scramble with Bobby Allison and Cale Yarborough, took the lead in the 1969 Rebel 400 with four laps to go after the trio tangled. Allison bounced off the outside wall into Yarborough, and both went spinning off the track. Allison wound up stopped against a concrete wall, while LeeRoy Yarbrough spun his car around and kept going. He went on to win the race with Cale second, Allison third, Paul Goldsmith fourth and David Pearson fifth.

With the new asphalt on the track and the new banking in turns three and four, Cale established a track record in qualifying, averaging 152.293 mph – the first time a car had ever averaged more than 150 mph at the egg-shaped oval.

(Left) In 1965, Bob Colvin welcomed to Darlington Raceway television stars Ken Curtis (Festus) and Milburn Stone (Doc) from the hit show "Gunsmoke."

(Below) Frank Sutton, otherwise known as Sergeant Carter on the hit television series "Gomer Pyle," horses around with driver Tiny Lund prior to the 1968 Southern 500.

Actor Clint Eastwood "made his day" by being the Grand Marshal for the 1963 Southern 500, and jumped behind the wheel of the pace car.

Labor Day was a different story for LeeRoy Yarbrough, but the ending was the same.

In a rain-shortened event cut to 316 miles, it all came down to a 30-lap shootout between Pearson and Yarbrough. Pearson's team took on a soft-compound tire that would give him more speed, but only for a short period of time. Yarbrough's team opted for a harder tire, which would be better for the long haul.

With 10 laps to go, Pearson shot past Yarbrough and pulled away. But ever so slightly, Yarbrough began to reel him in. Pearson's car was skating up the track in the corners and Yarbrough was a man on a mission.

On the final turn of the final lap, Yarbrough shot under Pearson in the third turn, made the pass, and held on for a bumper-to-bumper victory.

"My car was pushing so hard, I finally hit the fence in that third turn when he passed me," said Pearson afterwards.

LeeRoy Yarbrough was the talk of Darlington – and NASCAR – in 1969. He wrote his own page in the NASCAR history book by becoming the first driver to win NASCAR's triple crown: the Daytona 500, the World 600 in Charlotte and the Southern 500 in the same year.

The decade of the 1960s was a time of change and growth in the sport. The cars were faster because the technology was better. Cars were made safer by NASCAR standards, and new heroes were made like Richard Petty, David Pearson, Fred Lorenzen, Cale Yarborough, Junior Johnson and Bobby Allison.

New superspeedways were built in Michigan, Charlotte, Atlanta, Rockingham (N.C.) and Talladega (Ala.). But Darlington, the track that started it all, continued to flourish. It, too, was growing – adding new grandstands, updating buildings and reworking the track to make for better competition.

The festive atmosphere at Darlington continued. Celebrities like Hollywood stars Clint Walker, Clint Eastwood, Frank Sutton (Sergeant Carter) from "Gomer Pyle," and George Lyndsey (Goober) from the Andy Griffith Show were a part of the history, the tradition and the nostalgia of Darlington. By the end of the decade, almost every character on "Gunsmoke" had appeared at Darlington. Ken Curtis of "Festus" fame and Miblurn "Doc" Stone joined James (Matt Dillon) Arness in branding the track "Too Tough To Tame."

KEEP THE MONEY AT HOME

NASCAR racing was changing dramatically when the 1970 season began. Speeds were higher than ever, expenses were higher than ever and the cars on the tracks bore no resemblance to the family sedans first driven by race drivers into Darlington's garage area.

The winter of the previous year had been filled with controversy. Car manufacturers were trying to dictate rules, new speedway operators were trying to break NASCAR President Bill France's hold on the sport, and drivers were looking for more prize money and benefits.

By the time the dust settled, France remained solidly in control and had negotiated a network television contract with ABC for $1.365 million, with a portion of the money going to the tracks, a portion going to the drivers via the race purses, and a portion being disbursed to those tracks not included in the televised schedule.

Darlington's Rebel 400 was one of the televised races, and Richard Petty provided a spectacular accident that went into the living rooms of millions of Americans shortly after the live coverage on ABC began.

On the 176th lap of the 291-lap (400-mile) race, Petty's car lost traction off the

(Above) An aerial view of the Darlington Raceway during the 1970s.

(Right) For years, Chris Economaki, the dean of broadcasters and publisher emeritus of National Speed Sport News, covered events at Darlington for ABC Sports. Here, he's perched on top of a stack of Goodyear tires.

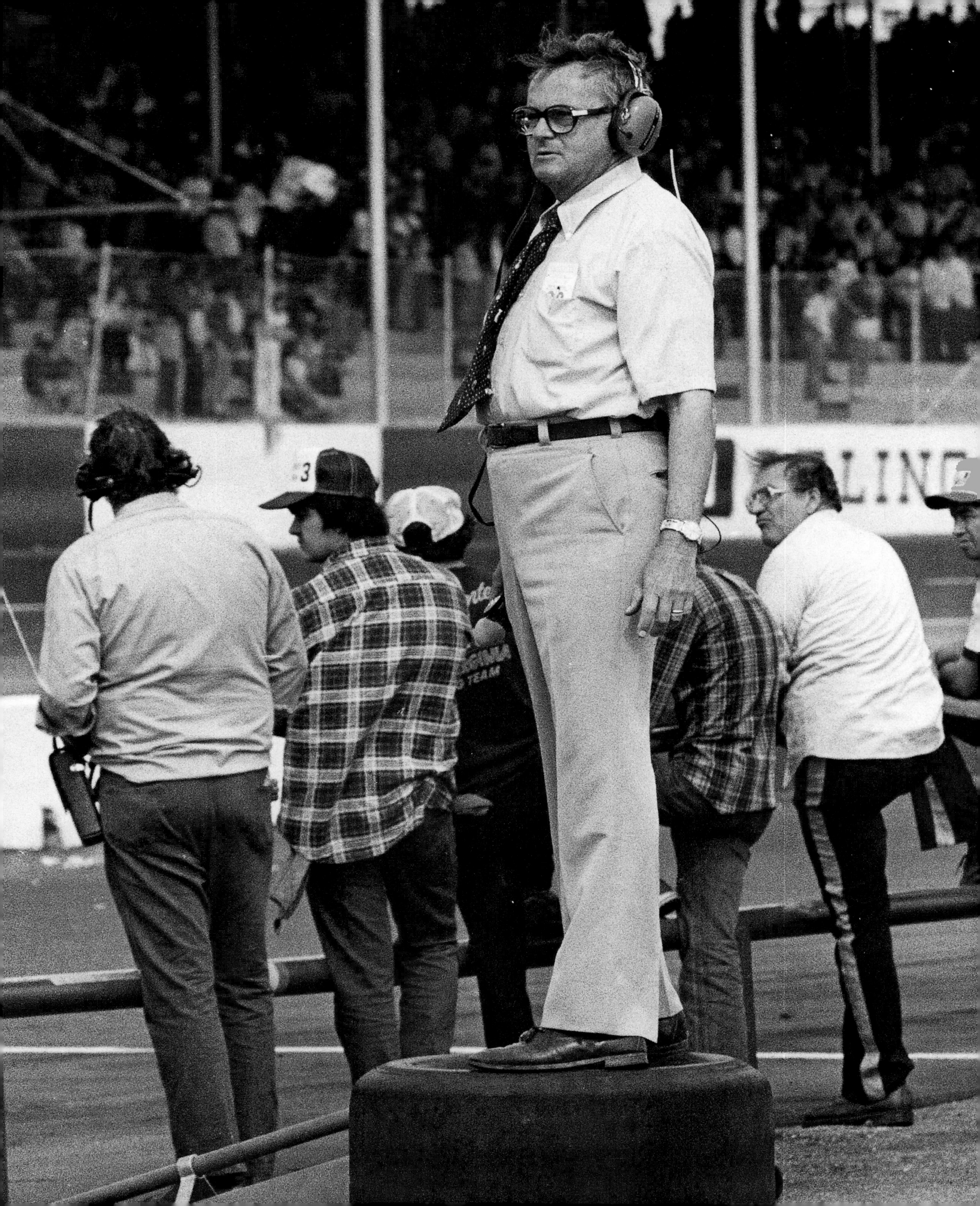

fourth turn, turned over several times and crashed into the inside concrete wall, scattering debris and pieces everywhere. Petty was removed, unconscious, from his Plymouth Superbird and transported to a Florence hospital where he regained consciousness and was diagnosed only with a broken shoulder.

"That wreck looked a lot worse than a broken shoulder," said eyewitness Mike Harkey, who watched in disbelief as Petty's car pitched and tumbled violently through the air. "Everyone thought Richard had to be hurt bad - real bad."

Petty himself dismissed the entire incident in typical Petty fashion saying, "I don't know what it looked like. I was knocked out, so I missed the whole deal. It shore tore up my car, though."

Actually, this particular race week at Darlington had been anything but kind to Petty. He also had demolished a car during practice leading up to race day.

While it was definitely a bad week for King Richard, it was a good week for David Pearson, who lapped the field three times en route his Rebel 400 victory. Dick Brooks from Porterville, Calif., finished second and eventual 1970 NASCAR Champion Bobby Isaac was third.

Pearson drove a Holman-Moody Ford, while Brooks drove a Plymouth Superbird and Isaac piloted a Dodge Daytona. Rounding out the top 10 were James Hylton (Ford), Benny Parsons (Ford), Buddy Arrington (Dodge), Dr. Don Tarr (Dodge), Roy Mayne (Chevrolet), Jabe Thomas (Plymouth) and Bill Dennis (Chevrolet).

It was Pearson's second trip to victory lane at Darlington, but his feel for the track would provide record-setting results in the years to come. "I don't know exactly what it is about Darlington, but I've always liked it," said Pearson. "You have to be patient at Darlington and take what the track gives you. You can't force things."

While Pearson had a passion for racing at Darlington, one of his closest friends in the sport, fellow driver Bobby Isaac, absolutely despised the track. "I wouldn't care if they plowed this place up and planted peanuts or soybeans or whatever they had growing here before they built a race track," said Isaac. "I absolutely hate this place, and it sure as hell don't like me none, either."

Isaac never won at Darlington and certainly wasn't the only stock car driver, or race car driver for that matter, to develop an ongoing dislike for the toughest, oldest paved track in NASCAR. While Isaac's love-hate relationship came up every time he raced at Darlington, the 1970 Southern 500 would go down in history as the year Isaac almost tamed this tiger of a track.

The "King" on his throne at Darlington. Richard Petty collected three Darlington wins in his career - two in the Rebel 400, and the 1967 Southern 500.

After claiming the 1971 Southern 500, Bobby Allison gets a shower of soda as wife Judy and car owner Ralph Moody look on.

Had it not been for a bit of pit strategy that backfired, Isaac might have been in a position to challenge race winner Buddy Baker down the stretch, but Baker's victory was a storybook finish of its own.

Baker had been to victory lane at Darlington before, but not as a driver. He was there with his father, Buck Baker, winner of three Southern 500 races (1953, 1960, 1964), and it had been a lifelong dream of Buddy's to make it to Darlington's victory lane as a driver.

Actually, young Buddy did it in convincing fashion, putting his Cotton Owens-prepared Dodge across the finish line a full lap ahead of Isaac and third-place finisher Pete Hamilton. Four laps back was Pearson, and Richard Petty was fifth, another lap back.

Baker was exuberant in victory lane. "This is a race I've been wanting to win since I was nine years old," he said. "I might just be the happiest man in the world."

Owens, crew chief and car owner, was pretty happy himself. The ex-driver turned car owner had been inducted into the National Motorsports Press Association Hall of Fame earlier that weekend. "What a great way to cap this weekend," said Owens.

From a Darlington Raceway perspective, the 1971 season was extremely important because the sport as a whole was tiptoeing through one of those years that journalist Bob Talbert would have termed "succeeding in spite of itself."

Ford factory support was withdrawn. Carburetor plates were introduced. Chrysler was unhappy. And Bill France, to insure sufficient fields of cars for the short-track races, announced plans to allow the NASCAR Grand American (small cars) Division to compete in the Grand National (NASCAR Winston Cup Series) events. Martinsville President Clay Earles publicly denounced such plans and said he would run Grand National cars only. Actually, it was not the first time Earles and France would disagree, but the two pioneers would stand up together whenever the

sport came under attack from any outsider.

Both men agreed that the addition of Winston as title sponsor during the 1971 season would help build the credibility of the sport, particularly with the announcement of Winston's $100,000 contribution to a special point fund, as well as billboard and print advertising in support of selected events. Winston also announced sponsorship of one of the races at Talladega, which is now recognized as one of the premier races on the circuit, the Winston 500 at Talladega Superspeedway.

Darlington Raceway President Barnie Wallace, who took over following Bob Colvin's death in 1967, worked diligently throughout the winter months between the 1970 and 1971 seasons to make a much-needed change that would help the Raceway for years to come. He enlisted the aid of local politicians to allow the Raceway to legally hold events on Sunday. With the help of young Darlington attorney and member of the South Carolina House of Representatives John P. Gardner Jr., Darlington Raceway scheduled and held its first "legal" Sunday race. (Previously, South Carolina's Blue Laws forbid retail activities on Sundays.)

Buddy Baker appeared to make a shambles of the com-

Buddy Baker and car owner Cotton Owens look over their Dodge prior to the 1970 Southern 500.

petition in the first Rebel 400 run on Sunday, winning by seven laps. But Baker's Dodge went to the front just 11 laps from the finish when Donnie Allison's Mercury began to sputter. Allison had been the dominant force in the race to that point.

Dick Brooks wound up second with Dave Marcis third. Allison nursed his sick machine home in fourth and Jim Vandiver finished fifth. Rounding out the top 10 were G.C. Spencer, J.D. McDuffie, Friday Hassler, Ben Arnold and Elmo Langley.

David Pearson quit the Holman-Moody team following his exit from the race with steering problems after just 30 laps. The Spartanburg driver, however, would return to the circuit later, very much a contender.

Fred Lorenzen, the one-time "Golden Boy" of Ford Motor Company came out of retirement in 1971 to give the Southern 500 one last shot. Lorenzen, mounted in a Wood Brothers Ford capable of winning, drove the car with reckless abandon during practice, pushing it further and further into the corners. During his qualifying attempt, the tough old track took a bite out of Lorenzen. Fearless Freddie spun off turn four, bounced off the outside wall and slammed the inside retaining

South Carolina's Cotton Owens of Spartanburg, ran in the first Southern 500 in 1950, but didn't get his first win at the track "Too Tough To Tame" until 1970 as a car owner for Buddy Baker.

429 C.I.
GOODYEAR
PROVEN by holman moody
Purolator
Regal Ride
GOODYEAR
Purolator
Purolator
Purolator
Purolator

The Wood Brothers were famous for lightning fast pit stops with David Pearson behind the wheel. Here, Pearson receives service in the 1972 Rebel 400 on the way to the win.

wall. The incident sent him to the hospital with multiple injuries including a broken foot and numerous lacerations. He recovered from his injuries, but Lorenzen did not compete in the '71 Southern 500.

This particular Southern 500 belonged to Bobby Allison and his Holman-Moody Mercury, and Allison left no doubt in the minds of the fans who attended the event. Allison started from the pole position and led 329 of the 367 laps, beating Richard Petty to the finish line by more than a lap. Buddy Baker was third, Bobby Isaac fourth and Dave Marcis came home in fifth.

James Hylton wound up sixth and country music star Marty Robbins was seventh. Robbins, a favorite with NASCAR fans and extremely popular in the garage area, dabbled in racing when his schedule permitted. He was a regular at Nashville Speedway, where he would make an early appearance at the Grand Old Opry, and then rush out to the Raceway to run the feature.

The race rundown for the 1971 Southern 500 revealed a big difference in the "have's" and "have-not's" regarding financial support for race teams. The first four finishers - Allison, Petty, Baker and Isaac - were amongst the "have's."

The rest of the finishing field, including Marcis and Robbins belonged to the "have-not's." This list also included John Sears, Cecil Gordon, Roy Mayne, Ben Arnold, Henley Gray, Earl Brooks, Raymond Williams, Eddie Yarboro, Benny Parsons (who had some sponsorship assistance from L.G. DeWitt, one of the owners of North Carolina Motor Speedway), Ed Negre, Larry Baumel, Bill Dennis (who was driving for Junie Donlavey at the time), Wendell Scott (the only African-American to win a NASCAR Winston Cup Series event), G.C. Spencer, Dean Dalton, Joe Frasson, Charlie Glotzbach (who was driving an independently-owned Chevrolet for Charlotte Motor Speedway owner Richard Howard), Dick May, Earl Champion (a Virginia short-track veteran whose No. 10 inspired fellow Virginian Ricky Rudd to use the number years later), Marv Acton, Bill Shirey, Walter Ballard, Pete Hamilton (who was driving for Cotton Owens at the time), Frank Warren, Bill Seifert, Friday Hassler, Elmo Langley, Pearson (who was driving for flash-in-the pan Chris Vallo),

After David Pearson (left) won the 1977 Southern 500, he was joined in victory lane by the Rookie of the Race, Ricky Rudd, who finished seventh, and Darlington Raceway President Barney Wallace.

(Above) In 1976, Strom Thurmond (left) along with Bob Dole, joined Richard Petty and his father, Lee, prior to the start of a race at Darlington. Dole was running for President that year.

(Right) Winston's Ralph Seagraves tours the Darlington garage with Billy Carter, brother of former United States President Jimmy Carter, in the late 1970s.

Bobby Mausgrover, Neil Castles, Jabe Thomas, Dick Brooks and J.D. McDuffie.

Picking a winner was fairly easy since a few teams were so much better equipped and better prepared than others, including Petty, who won 23 of the 46 events he started during the season, which helped him capture the 1971 championship.

In 1972, Big Bill turned the reins of NASCAR over to his oldest son William C. France Jr., the same son who had come up through the ranks of NASCAR cutting grass, driving a race car, selling tickets, directing traffic, digging ditches, building buildings, routing sewer lines, parking cars, selling snow cones and just about anything else that needed to be done over the years.

The NASCAR Winston Cup Series schedule also underwent significant changes for the 1972 season, with NASCAR eliminating many of the short-track events. The schedule would now consist of 31 races, including, of course, Darlington's Rebel 400 in the spring and the traditional Southern 500 on Labor Day weekend.

By the time the teams left Darlington this time around, a dynasty was in the works. David Pearson teamed up with the Wood Brothers for the Rebel 400, and Pearson proved

(Above) The Silver Fox, David Pearson, is Darlington's all-time best.

(Right) The Wood Brothers Racing Team won eight races at Darlington, including the 1976 Rebel 500 with David Pearson at the wheel. That's Leonard Wood to the left of Pearson, while Glenn Wood is on Pearson's right. Sharing in the excitement is David's son Eddie and Kim Wood, daughter of Leonard Wood.

on qualifying day that he had what it takes to win. He put the maroon-white-and-gold Mercury on the pole position with a speed of 148.209 miles per hour and went on to win the race by a little over a lap. Richard Petty was second and Joe Frasson was third. Benny Parsons finished fourth and James Hylton was fifth.

The victory was sort of poetic justice for Pearson, who hadn't won a race since quitting the Holman-Moody team several years earlier. "I guess there were people who thought I was over the hill when I quit Holman-Moody, and Bobby Allison won races in the Holman-Moody car. But I never doubted myself, and we were just in sort of a bad situation, where we never could get anything going with the Chris Vallo team. I knew I could still get the job done."

Pearson almost made it a Darlington sweep in the Southern 500 but, as he put it afterwards, "I just got my fanny whipped!" He was referring to Bobby Allison's victory in the Labor Day Classic.

Allison, driving one of those Richard Howard Chevrolets, dueled with Pearson throughout the event, racing side by side at times, before Allison took the lead for good just six laps from the finish. The dueling pair finished seven laps in front of third-place finisher Richard Petty. Darlington fans cheered Allison and Pearson throughout the event as they swapped the lead back and forth more than a dozen times.

Taking a back seat to this dynamic duo was none other than Fred Lorenzen, in yet another comeback attempt trying to win the Southern 500 in a Chevrolet prepared by Hoss Ellington. Lorenzen managed to bring the car home fourth, more than a dozen laps back, and several laps ahead of fifth-place finisher H.B. Bailey. It was Lorenzen's last hurrah at Darlington Raceway.

Buddy Arrington, Dave Marcis, Jim Vandiver, Marty Robbins and Coo Coo Marlin, father of 1990s star Sterling Marlin, rounded out the top 10. It was Robbins' second top-10 finish at Darlington in as many races.

Just how good were Pearson and the Wood Brothers? Well, Pearson won the Rebel 500 at Darlington in 1973 by 13 laps. It was the biggest margin of victory since Ned Jarrett won the 1965 Southern 500 by a whopping 14 laps.

After the 1979 Rebel 500, David Pearson and the Wood Brothers team split, but Pearson came back to Darlington later that year subbing for an injured rookie named Dale Earnhardt in the Southern 500. The result was Pearson picking up his ninth Darlington triumph. Track President Barney Wallace presents the trophy while crew chief Jake Elder (right) and Miss Southern 500 Renee Rodrique look on.

Pearson also won 10 other races during the season, including the Carolina 500 at Rockingham, the Atlanta 500, the Virginia 500 at Martinsville (right down the road from the Wood Brothers Stuart, Va., complex), the Winston 500 at Talladega, the Mason-Dixon 500 at Dover, the Motor State 400 at Michigan, the Firecracker 400 at Daytona, the Dixie 500 at Atlanta, the Delaware 500 at Dover and the American 500 at Rockingham.

Actually, Pearson's victory in the Rebel 500 was a landmark of another sort, besides being so lopsided. It was the first time the spring race at Darlington was scheduled for 500 miles. Heretofore, it had been a 300-miler, originally, and then a 400-miler.

Pearson, however, was the lone driver to go the new 500-mile distance. He took the lead on the 190th lap of the 367-lap event and kept it the rest of the way. The only driver who might have challenged him at the end, Bobby Allison, fell out of contention with engine problems after completing 349 laps. Allison still finished third behind Pearson and runner-up Benny Parsons. Richard Childress was fourth behind Allison, and J.D. McDuffie finished in fifth.

Parsons' runner-up finish was a feat in itself, as Benny had to nurse a torn-up race car around Darlington's treacherous,

Benny Parsons doesn't care if he gets a soaking wet bath from his crew chief Jake Elder. Why? Because he just won at Darlington (the 1978 Rebel 500).

egg-shaped oval for the final 30 miles or so, after being involved in a multi-car accident on the front straightaway.

Cale Yarborough won his second Southern 500 in 1973, beating Pearson by a half lap in his Junior Johnson-prepared, Richard Howard-owned Chevrolet. Cale had left the NASCAR circuit several seasons earlier when the factories pulled out of NASCAR and tried his hand at Indianapolis-type racing. He drove for former NASCAR driver turned Indy car owner Gene White, who fielded Indy cars for veteran Lloyd Ruby of Wichita Falls, Texas.

Cale actually earned a top-10 finish in the Indianapolis 500, but jumped at the chance to get back into NASCAR when the 1973 season started. Having been off the NASCAR radar screen for a while, many in the sport didn't think Cale could win again. Little did they know, Yarborough not only would win, but he also would become a solid contender for a number of years, ultimately winning three consecutive NASCAR championships (1976-78).

The 1973 Southern 500 victory was particularly pleasing to Cale, one of the most tenacious drivers in NASCAR history. Runner-up Pearson paid Yarborough the highest of compliments following his victory. "I thought I might have a chance late in the race," said Pearson, "but when it came time to go, Cale took off. I just couldn't keep up with him."

Buddy Baker wound up third, a lap off the blistering pace, and Richard Petty was five laps further back in fourth. Parsons was fifth, Bobby Allison sixth, Coo Coo Marlin seventh, Darrell Waltrip eighth, Dick Brooks ninth and J.D. McDuffie took 10th place.

The Raceway, with Barnie Wallace at the helm, made several improvements during this period, building a new garage, a new cafeteria and new buildings for Goodyear and Unocal in the garage area. Wallace, a quiet, unassuming gentleman, was one of the original shareholders when Harold Brasington first began selling shares. He was very frugal, and the Darlington Raceway stockholders reaped the rewards of dividend checks every year he was in control.

"Harold came by the store one day (Wallace owned and operated a country store near Hartsville and Darlington before getting involved with the track full time) and painted a glowing picture," recalled Wallace years later. "He wanted me to invest $5,000 and promised me I'd get it back after the first race. I knew I was crazy, but I had attended some races in the Carolinas and I really liked it. When I went to the building and loan association to withdraw the money, the officer asked me what in the world I was going to do with such a large sum of money. I told him I was going to invest it in Harold's race track. He assured me I was going to lose that, and much more."

Although quiet - almost to a fault in what would become such a gregarious business - Wallace surrounded himself with outgoing people. His friend and longtime Raceway supporter Walter D. (Red) Tyler, Darlington attorney Robert Kilgo, J.K. "Scrunt" Schipman, St. John's High School (in Darlington) football coach Jim "Weepy" Welch, Floyd Lane and public relations director Bill Kiser all helped Wallace keep the track in the limelight.

Kiser, a former sports reporter, was a "wheeler-dealer" of the first order and used his talents to make sure Darlington was included in conversations regarding NASCAR and stock car racing. The popular Kiser served as executive secretary of the National Motorsports Press Association, which allowed him to keep his fingers on the pulse of the sport.

A highlight of Benny Parsons' career came when he won the 1978 Rebel 500. Just right of Benny is crew chief Jake Elder, and at the far right is L.G. Dewitt, car owner and former owner of North Carolina Speedway.

Kiser's energy, along with that of everyone else involved in NASCAR racing during 1974, was directed at fuel consumption. This was the year of the energy crisis, and stock car racing was an obvious target as people lined up at service stations to make sure they had enough gas to get to work and back.

Following NASCAR President Bill France's lead to comply with energy consumption cutbacks, Darlington's Rebel 500 became the Rebel 450, and David Pearson proved to be just as good no matter the distance of a Darlington race. At the end of the 330-lap event, Pearson's Wood Brothers Mercury crossed the finish line ahead of Bobby Allison, Buddy Baker, Donnie Allison and Cale Yarborough.

Bobby Allison felt the energy crunch a little more than others in the field. The Alabama driver ran out of gas on the final lap. Allison led much of the final 50 miles before Pearson passed him with just 11 laps to go. Pearson fans credited the Silver Fox's patience in saving fuel for the victory.

Cale Yarborough survived the 1974 Labor Day classic to capture his third Southern 500 crown. And, "survived" is the only way to put it. Only 12 cars were around at the finish on a day of demolition. The tough, old Darlington track bit all but a few of the favorites, including Pearson, Benny Parsons, Buddy Baker, Richard Petty, Charlie Glotzbach, Bobby Allison and Jim Vandiver. Of the cars that weren't involved in accidents, 13 went to the garage with engine failures.

Before he ever competed at Darlington, a young Kyle Petty (right) was on his father's pit crew, joining crew chief Dale Inman.

Ol' D.W., Darrell Waltrip, served as the Grand Marshal for the Southern 500 Parade on the streets of downtown Darlington. That's his wife, Stevie, alongside, while the jeep is being driven by track President Barney Wallace.

"The Good Lord just looked after me today," said Cale afterwards. "I don't know how I missed all the wrecks but I'm sure glad I did."

It was Bobby Allison back in the winner's circle at Darlington in the 1975 Rebel 500, after David Pearson and Benny Parsons hit the first-turn wall while racing for the lead. Allison also came back to win the Southern 500, completing a sweep of Darlington for the year.

The real kicker is that Allison was driving a Matador - an American Motors car about as slick-looking as an overseas cargo container. One writer described Allison and his Matador this way: "Sending Bobby Allison out on the race track in that Matador to compete against Fords, Chevrolets, Dodges and the likes, is like sending home-run king Hank Aaron to the plate without his bat!" Allison, nonetheless, hit two home runs in the toughest ballpark on the NASCAR circuit in 1975.

The remainder of the 1970s at Darlington belonged to big names in the sport. And heading the list was Pearson. He won both races in 1976, won the Southern 500 in 1977 and came back to win the 1979 Southern 500 as a relief driver for injured rookie Dale Earnhardt. Pearson's Southern 500 win in 1976 gave him the distinction of winning the sport's Triple Crown as the Spartanburg native also captured the Daytona 500 and Charlotte World 600 prior to Labor Day.

Cale Yarborough won another Southern 500 in 1978, while Darrell Waltrip put his name in the Darlington record book with a pair of Rebel 500 wins (1977 and 1979). Benny Parsons also became a Darlington winner with a win in the 1978 Rebel 500.

In the 1979 Rebel 500, Pearson ended his seven-year relationship with the Wood Brothers after a much-publicized pit-road incident when a lack of communication resulted in Pearson pulling away from his pit stall before the lug nuts had been tightened. The result was the famed Wood Brothers Mercury flopping around at the end of pit road like a hooked flounder, while the left-side tires rolled slowly away from the car.

Actually, it was a bizarre scene since the Wood Brothers team had built a reputation over the years as the fastest pit crew in the world. Pearson thought the crew was going to change only two tires and was anxious to get back on the track, as he was in contention for another win. Crew chief Leonard Wood was yelling, "Whoa! Whoa!" But Pearson thought he was yelling, "Go! Go!"

Pearson gained some measure of revenge for the embarrassing incident later in the year with his third Southern 500 victory, but not before Waltrip suffered his own embarrassment. Waltrip spun out twice within 10 laps, which opened the door for Pearson's win.

Waltrip said afterwards, "I feel like the little boy who dreads going home because he knows he ought to get a spanking when he gets there."

Actually, Waltrip deserved his self-induced punishment for only the first of his two spinouts. "The first one was driver error," he said. "The second was tire failure. I must have cut a tire but dad-gummed if it wasn't in almost exactly the same spot as I had spun the first time."

Waltrip shrugged and grinned, "Oh well, that's Darlington, isn't it?

MILLION DOLLAR BILL

When the 1980 NASCAR Winston Cup Series season began with Speedweeks in Daytona, David Pearson, one of the sport's all-time winners, was watching from the sidelines without a ride. Some folks were saying he was finished.

Those who knew him, knew better.

"If the right deal comes along, I'll drive," said Pearson, whose career had spanned nearly 20 years, during which he had won three NASCAR championships (1966, 1968 and 1969). Actually, those three years were the only years Pearson ran for the championship as he didn't like all the travel, leading one to ponder if there is another driver who won the championship every year he chased it.

Pearson was comfortable. He didn't think he had anything to prove. If there's ever been a what-you-see-is-what-you-get kind of person, David Pearson is it. No frills. No fancy words. No briefcase. No put-on. Just plain old David. And, he'll resent being referred to as "old." ("That's all in your mind," he'll say.)

David, winner of NASCAR's Triple Crown in 1976 (Daytona 500, World 600 and Southern 500), was just hanging around in Daytona, looking at the cars,

(Above) Relief times two: Richard Petty called on Donnie Allison to relief-drive after suffering from the heat during the 1980 Southern 500. Allison (exiting the car) experienced back pain after straining to reach the pedals, so Neil Bonnett was called in as third driver of the STP entry.

(Right) David Pearson (left) and Wood Brothers crew chief Leonard Wood teamed up for many victories until their breakup following Darlington's 1979 CRC Rebel 500.

GOOD YEA

talking to his friends and keeping an ear out for the right kind of ride. But nothing happened.

Unfazed, Pearson returned home to Spartanburg, where he tinkered around in his shop, mowed the lawn, spent time with the boys (Larry, Eddie and Ricky), ate breakfast with Bud Moore and some of the other guys he'd been meeting for breakfast for years, and generally enjoyed life.

"It wasn't the end of the world for me," said Pearson.

Then, why in the world would he show up at Darlington in April for the CRC Rebel 500 as the driver of Hoss Ellington's car?

"Because I thought I could win," says Pearson, matter-of-factly. "And the deal was right!"

Pearson had already won the first NASCAR Late Model Sportsman (now called NASCAR Busch Series, Grand National Division) race ever held at Darlington Raceway the day before, beating Neil Bonnett and Dave Marcis to the finish line in a three-abreast, down-to-the-wire barn burner!

In fact, Pearson had won at Darlington many times before, most recently as a substitute for injured Dale Earnhardt in the previous year's Southern 500. Counting that victory, Pearson was Darlington's all-time winner with nine victories – and when he didn't win, he usually finished second.

Hoss Ellington and his former driver, Donnie Allison, had gone their separate ways a few weeks earlier, which prompted Hoss, one of NASCAR's most likeable characters, to give Pearson a call. Pearson got right down to business, putting Ellington's Hawaiian Tropic Chevrolet on the front row. Only Benny Parsons turned a faster qualifying lap in another Chevrolet.

"I knew Pearson didn't want to run a bunch of races and neither did I,' said Hoss, a former driver himself from Wilmington, N.C. "So I told David, let's do it! I'll have the car ready for you at Darlington."

Pearson took the car to the front on the first lap and held it there until young, hard-charging Dale Earnhardt slid past him on lap 14. Typically Pearson, he kept the leaders in sight. This was the Silver Fox at his best, sliding back in the field and taking care of his equipment, hoping to be able to make a charge at the end.

As Darrell Waltrip put it, "You'd see Pearson at the start of the race and then he'd disappear. You'd figure he fell out of the race. Then, with 50 miles or so to go, here he'd come, passing you like you was standing still and you'd say to yourself, 'Where in the dickens did he come from?'"

A bad thunderstorm (which pelted the track with hail)

Terry Labonte celebrates his only Darlington victory (1980) to date. Running fourth with just two laps remaining, Terry avoided oil on the track that eliminated the first three cars (Pearson, Earnhardt and Parsons) as they raced to the caution flag.

Dave Marcis' only trip to Darlington's victory lane to date came for winning the 1981 TranSouth 200, a Late Model Sportsman (now known as NASCAR Busch Grand National Series) race held the day before the TranSouth 500. Dave is shown here with wife Helen.

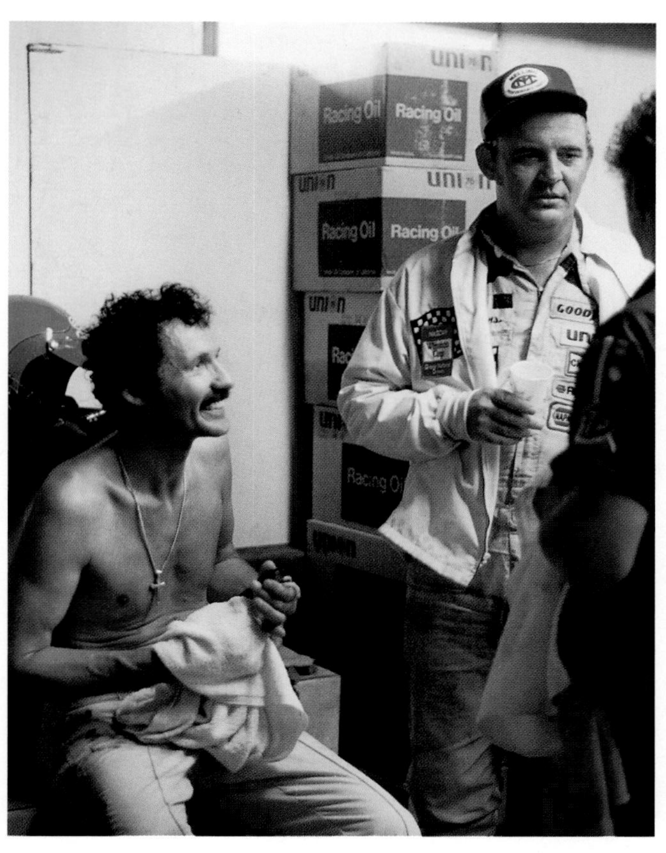

(Above) Only Benny Parsons (right) was faster than David Pearson in qualifying for the 1980 CRC Rebel 500. Between Parsons and Pearson, the front-row starters owned four NASCAR Winston Cup Series championships.

(Right) To commemorate his 1980 Southern 500 victory, Terry Labonte (right) is presented with this portrait by Darlington President Barney Wallace.

stopped the race before the halfway point. Approximately three hours later, NASCAR officials restarted the race, knowing darkness would fall before the completion of 500 miles. They informed all the teams the race would end five laps past the halfway point, and Pearson turned the jets on and took the checkered flag three seconds ahead of second-place Parsons. Pearson had his 10th Darlington victory and his 105th career win.

It was to be the last time Pearson visited a NASCAR Winston Cup Series victory lane, although he came close later in the 1980 season in the Labor Day Southern 500. Squeezing every ounce of speed from his Chevrolet to stay ahead of Dale Earnhardt, Benny Parsons and young sensation Terry Labonte, Pearson powered into Darlington's tight first turn with two laps remaining.

Just ahead of the charging pack, Frank Warren's Dodge blew an engine, spewing oil across the already-slick surface. Pearson's car hit the oil as though it was a banana peel, skidded sideways and scraped against the wall. Earnhardt and Parsons also spun.

During all the commotion, Labonte slipped past the entire group and made it back to the start-finish line in the lead, where he stayed while the race ended under caution. Pearson nursed his car across the line to finish second while Harry Gant passed Parsons to finish third. Parsons wound up fourth with Neil Bonnett fifth. Earnhardt dropped back to seventh behind Bobby Allison. It was a wild finish to a race during which 11 different drivers had the lead at one time or another, including Dale Earnhardt's future car owner, Richard Childress, one of the leading independent (meaning without significant sponsorship) drivers on the tour.

Sponsorship was playing a much bigger role in all aspects of the sport at the time. The TranSouth Financial Corporation joined Darlington Raceway as sponsor of the spring NASCAR Late Model Sportsman race. Several of the NASCAR Winston Cup Series teams were enjoying the fruits of sponsorship, as well.

Beer companies reached their target audiences by sponsoring both races and race cars. Bill Elliott's Coors Ford was joined in weekly on-track battles by cars sponsored by Budweiser, Miller and Old Milwaukee.

Richard Petty, of course, had STP and Hoss Ellington had Hawaiian Tropic, but there were others. Purolator was on board with the Wood Brothers, Gatorade with Darrell Waltrip and the DiGard team, Busch Beer sponsored Junior Johnson and Cale Yarborough, while Stratagraph (which was car owner Billy Hagan's company) supported Terry Labonte. M.C. Anderson provided backing for Benny Parsons, Truxmore for Junie Donlavey with driver Ricky Rudd, and CRC Chemicals put a little money behind Richard Childress' team.

These were not big sponsorships by today's standards, but progress was being made as many small business owners started making deals with car owners to put their business names on NASCAR race cars.

Harry Gant, shown here in 1981, won the '83 TranSouth 500 and '84 Southern 500.

Some of those in the 1980s included Native Tan, Frank Warren's sponsor for several years; Valvoline, who teamed up with M.C. Anderson at one time and also had arrangements with other teams; the orange-and-white Hardee's colors appeared on the cars of Cale Yarborough and Bobby Allison; and Wrangler Jeans combined with Dale Earnhardt and Richard Childress. Tim Richmond's car received sponsorship from the UNO card game, and even Apache Stoves got into the act, throwing support behind Benny Parsons at one point and, later, behind Mark Martin.

The beer companies took their marketing battles to the tracks in the 1980s with Busch, a longtime NASCAR sponsor, taking up with Junior Johnson and Cale Yarborough. Budweiser followed, also jumping in with Junior Johnson's team and drivers Darrell Waltrip, Terry Labonte and Geoff Bodine. Old Milwaukee threw their support behind Tim Richmond, Miller put their name on Bobby Allison's cars and Coors teamed up with Bill Elliott.

There were others as NASCAR racing broadened its marketing base. The product loyalty of NASCAR fans was catching on in boardrooms across America. Marketing experts raised their eyebrows and said, "Hey, the NASCAR fan buys products of companies supporting their sport! Let's get involved!"

U.S. Tobacco puts its smokeless tobacco band, Skoal, on a car owned by Hollywood stuntman Hal Needham and star Burt Reynolds, and hired Harry Gant to drive it. Gant became known as the "Skoal Bandit," a spin-off of Reynolds' starring role in the popular movie, "Smokey And The Bandit." U.S. Tobacco also put its Copenhagen brand on a car; Chattanooga Chew, another smokeless tobacco,

sponsored a car; as did Levi-Garrett, most noticeably with Geoffrey Bodine behind the wheel.

Does anyone remember Chameleon Sunglasses, sponsor of Junie Donlavey's car when Dick Brooks was the driver? How about Folgers Coffee with driver Tim Richmond? Zerex Antifreeze sponsored Alan Kulwicki; Bull Frog Knits was an associate on Buddy Baker's car; Underalls helped Sterling Marlin; and Kodak jumped in the sport with the McClure Racing Team. Kmart helped several teams; Quaker State sponsored a car; and Red Baron Frozen Pizza helped Ken Schrader's team.

When the teams rolled into Darlington for the 1981 CRC Chemicals Rebel 500, Junior Johnson's team carried Pepsi's Mountain Dew brand name on the side of the car driven by Darrell Waltrip. Darrell dominated the final 200 miles and held off Harry Gant down the stretch to win his first race at Darlington. It was also the first win for Buick at America's oldest superspeedway.

Darrell was hoping to make it two in a row at the Southern 500, but Neil Bonnett drove the Wood Brothers Ford home just in front of Waltrip's Buick. Dave Marcis was third in another Buick. Terry Labonte and Buddy Baker finished fourth and fifth, respectively, also in Buicks. Actually, 17 of the 40 cars in the starting field were Buicks for this race. Only Bobby Allison (9th) and Ricky Rudd (23rd) drove Chevrolets. Most of the General Motors teams opted for the Buick due to a narrower nose configuration.

By the time the 1982 NASCAR season rolled around, Darlington Raceway President Barney Wallace, Vice-President Walter D. (Red) Tyler and General Counsel Bob Kilgo were looking toward the future. Wallace had been diagnosed with cancer, Tyler was still helping his brothers run the Tyler Plywood Company in Florence on a daily basis and Kilgo was a lawyer, not a race promoter.

"No one in any of our families has any interest in operating a race track," said Wallace, "so we thought the best thing we could do was visit with the France family in Daytona Beach, and see if they might be interested in purchasing the track. We had a meeting with Bill France Jr., and the rest is history. We knew if the France family was involved, Darlington's place in the history of the sport would be okay."

While International Speedway Corporation's purchase of Darlington Raceway was still being negotiated, Wallace, Tyler and other Darlington officials hosted the 1982 CRC Chemicals Rebel 500. Once again, Bud Moore, the pioneer crew chief, engine builder and car owner, found himself in victory lane, this time with another one of those young hotshots at the wheel of his Ford, Dale Earnhardt from Kannapolis, N. C.

Young Earnhardt pushed his Ford past Cale Yarborough just 12 laps from the finish and captured his first Darlington victory. Over the next 15 years, Earnhardt's smiling face would be a regular in Darlington's victory lane, but the first one was special for the son of one of NASCAR's legendary pioneers, Ralph Earnhardt.

"I've always liked racing atDarlington and I always wanted to win here. This is one of my favorite tracks. It's tough – tougher than most tracks – but it's Darlington, and being tough is what makes it so special. I've had some bad luck here – blown motors, crashed, that kind of bad stuff –

As the NASCAR Winston Cup Series continued to grow, corporate America discovered the advantages of stock car sponsorship – illustrated here by Hardees (Yarborough) and U.S. Tobacco (Gant).

(Above) He must be hollering, because no one ever yawns after winning at Darlington. Neil Bonnett's 1981 Southern 500 win was his first and only Darlington victory.

(Left) Ray Melton – the voice of Darlington Raceway for many years – interviews Neil Bonnett (left) in victory lane.

but winning sure makes you forget the bad stuff . . . for a little while anyway," said Earnhardt after the victory, with that famous Earnhardt grin spreading across his face.

At this point in Earnhardt's career, he already had won the NASCAR Rookie of the Year title (1979) and, in his sophomore season, scored five victories on the way to the NASCAR Winston Cup Series championship. But the 1981 season proved to be winless for Earnhardt, and the Darlington victory was his only win in 1982. In spite of that, Dale had established himself as one of the favorites wherever he raced.

The 1982 Southern 500 had special significance. Back in June, the sale of the track had been completed, with International Speedway Corporation now the new owner. Barney Wallace remained as track president, and, although his health continued to decline, Wallace did everything within his power to make the 1982 Southern 500 bigger and better than ever.

Cale Yarborough, the homegrown little bull of a driver, put his name in the Darlington record book with an unprecedented fifth Southern 500 victory at the wheel of the M.C. Anderson-owned Buick. However, Richard Petty and Dale Earnhardt made Yarborough work for his record-breaking win.

Cale took the lead at lap 311 of the 367-lap distance, but Earnhardt charged past him at lap 341. Dale held on until Cale got past him again at lap 350. Six laps later, Petty passed Yarborough, with Earnhardt pressing hard. But Petty's lead lasted only four laps as Yarborough let it all hang out and passed Petty on the apron of turn three, sliding up the embankment and hanging on for dear life. Cale finished just ahead of Petty, with Earnhardt third, in what many fans still recall as one of the most exciting finishes in the history of NASCAR.

What better way to add to Darlington's tradition and history than to witness a "favorite son" winning his fifth Southern 500, adding to his victories in 1968, 1973, 1974 and 1978. This one, however, was "special, real special."

Cale had accomplished what no other driver had done. He had won stock car racing's most grueling race not once, like many drivers, not twice, like several drivers, not three times like Herb Thomas and Buck Baker, not four times like Bobby Allison (1971, 1972, 1975 and 1983), but an incredible five times!

One of the sport's truly nice guys, Harry Gant, won the

spring race in 1983 when race-leader Darrell Waltrip encountered engine problems two laps from the finish. "I couldn't believe it when I saw the smoke," said Gant. "He was sputtering and I just drove right on by."

Track President Barney Wallace died a few weeks following the 1983 TranSouth Financial 500 (the first year of a sponsorship arrangement that is still in effect today). Longtime Darlington Vice-President Walter D. (Red) Tyler was named track president. With Tyler at the helm, International Speedway Corporation began making numerous improvements,

(Above) Wrangler not only sponsored Dale Earnhardt's cars for a number of years, they also supplied pants for his pit crew, which showed how tough their jeans really were.

(Right) ABC-TV's Chris Economaki interviews Earnhardt in victory lane. The Rebel 500 win was Earnhardt's only victory of 1982.

(Below) Dale Earnhardt, in his pre-Intimidator era, accepts the 1982 CRC Rebel 500 trophy.

In recognition of his '81 Southern 500 triumph, Darlington Raceway President Barney Wallace presented Neil Bonnett this special Jeanne Barnes limited edition painting. The artwork then appeared on the cover of the 1982 Southern 500 program.

including new concrete walls, a control tower, new restrooms and new concession stands.

Bobby Allison won his fourth Southern 500 on Labor Day, beating Bill Elliott and Darrell Waltrip to the finish line. It was one of the hottest days in the history of the Southern 500 and Allison revealed after the race that his crew chief, Gary Nelson, had cut a hole in the roof of his Buick to cool Bobby off. "It was hot out there today." (Gary Nelson is now the NASCAR Winston Cup Series Director.)

Allison called it the "sweetest win of them all at this old place. I knew all we had to do was keep the car running those last few laps, but you never know when this old place is going to jump up and grab you. Was I near any trouble during the race today? Anytime you're racing at Darlington, you're near trouble, whether you know it or not!"

In winning the 1983 Southern 500, Allison will also always carry another distinction in his bag of NASCAR records: He won the last Southern 500 run on Labor Day Monday. NASCAR and Raceway officials agreed to move the race to Sunday over the holiday weekend, which would give fans a holiday (Monday) for travel. It would also give NASCAR an extra day to race should inclement weather prohibit racing on Sunday.

Darlington underwent a substantial facelift in 1984. Here the old pagoda makes way for new structures at NASCAR's oldest superspeedway.

Raceway President Red Tyler rebuilt Darlington's pit road during the winter between the 1983 and 1984 seasons, and told all the teams, in typical Tyler style, "Pit road's gonna be as smooth as a baby's behind when ya'll come back here next spring."

Tyler's wit and personality were widely known and respected throughout NASCAR circles. Red never met a stranger, and his southern twang and drawl would light up the darkest room. He was never at a loss for jokes or "demeaning" comments, sometimes aimed at himself or his wife, Marge, of "two-thousand years," as Red used to say, affectionately known in racing circles as "Miss Margie."

He was a solid businessman and had worked with both Bob Colvin and Barney Wallace for many years in overseeing the business side of racing. He also served on the South Carolina Pardon and Parole Board for nearly 20 years, many of those as Chairman.

Tyler took down the old infield pagoda in 1984 and built a new control tower and Motor Racing Network (MRN) booth atop the Colvin Grandstand (named for former President Bob Colvin) along the front straightaway. In fact, all the grandstands at the track were named after former track presidents. The fourth turn "covered" grandstand (now the second turn), originally known as the Robert E. Lee Paddock, was renamed Brasington Grandstand.

"We kept things pretty simple in the early days," said Clarice Lane with a chuckle. "The grandstand on the front side of the track was called Grandstand A, and the grandstand on the back side was called Grandstand B. Then, Grandstand A became Colvin, Grandstand B became Wallace (after Barney Wallace), the Robert E. Lee Paddock became Brasington (after Harold Brasington) and Red Tyler told me they named the newest infield restroom the "Clarice Lane Pit Stop." Clarice said she actually rode inside the track to make sure Red hadn't put up such a sign on the side of the rest room.

If Darrell Waltrip had been able to put a sign up during the 1984 TranSouth 500, it would have read: "Danger! Hungry Piranhas Feeding!"

"That's what it was like out there today," Waltrip said after winning a crash-filled event that eliminated more than one-fourth of the starting field. "It was like a bunch

Bob Colvin's wife Loomis (right) stands with track president Barney Wallace prior to the dedication of the Bob Colvin Grandstand in the early '80s. The grandstand was named for Darlington's second president.

Veteran D.K. Ulrich takes a wild ride after crashing with Rookie of the Year contenders Rusty Wallace (88) and Greg Sacks (51). Also involved were Geoff Bodine (5) and Dick Brooks.

of hungry piranhas in a pool trying to get at one little piece of meat."

The first crash ended any chance of victory for Richard Petty, along with Bobby Allison, Dick Brooks and Ron Bouchard. Later on, Geoff Bodine, Greg Sacks, Rusty Wallace and D.K. Ulrich tangled. On top of all that, Tim Richmond spun twice.

Said Waltrip, who finished ahead of Terry Labonte, Bill Elliott, Cale Yarborough and Dale Earnhardt, "It's a miracle anybody finished, including me. Man, was it wild out there today!

"The thing you have to keep telling yourself when you race at Darlington is to race the track, not the other guys. Guys who lose their temperament here are gonna lose the race, as well. You gotta be cool to win at Darlington."

Harry Gant won the first Southern 500 held on a Sunday (Sept. 2, 1984). "Handsome Harry" kept his Chevrolet out front for most of the afternoon to out-distance Tim Richmond, Buddy Baker, Rusty Wallace and Ricky Rudd. Dick Brooks finished sixth, followed by Phil Parsons, Terry Labonte, Benny Parsons and winner of the last Southern 500 held on Labor Day, Bobby Allison.

Bill Elliott had become a contender in the NASCAR Winston Cup Series prior to the 1985 season. He had won a

few races, and the Elliott Brothers were beginning to jell a little bit. Driving for owner Harry Melling with Coors as a sponsor, Elliott's Ford Thunderbird hit Daytona's Speedweeks like a speeding bullet.

Lean, lanky Bill, with a crop of red hair and a genuine, boy-next-door smile, smoked the competition in the season-opening Daytona 500. By the time the NASCAR Winston Cup Series hit Darlington for the TranSouth 500 in April, Elliott was the overwhelming favorite to win.

True-to-form, he started first and finished first, lapping all but two of his competitors – Darrell Waltrip and Tim Richmond. It was Elliott's first win at Darlington, but it would not be the most memorable. The second time around – the 1985 Southern 500 – would be worth an extra million dollars!

As Darlington President Red Tyler put it, "Most stock car drivers will run over each other for a few bucks! What do you think they're going to do for a million bucks? Shoot, I'd run over my two brothers for a million bucks," Tyler added with a laugh. "Worse than that, they'd sho' 'nuff run over me!"

The million-dollar bonus program came from Series sponsor Winston. Prior to the 1985 season, R.J. Reynolds President and Chief Executive Officer Jerry Long, a

favorite amongst NASCAR officials and teams for his company's longtime support and genuine interest in the sport, announced at the annual NASCAR Winston Cup Series Awards Banquet, a new program for 1985 to be sponsored by the Winston brand. The program would put up a $1 million bonus to any driver who could win three of four specific events on the NASCAR Winston Cup Series schedule.

The four races were the Daytona 500 (the biggest of all NASCAR races), the Winston 500 at Talladega (the fastest), the World 600 at Charlotte (the longest), and the Southern 500 at Darlington Raceway (the oldest, the most historic and the race with the most tradition of all NASCAR races).

In the first year of this million-dollar deal, popular Elliott had started his season with a win in the Daytona 500. In late July, he scored an unbelievable win in Talladega's Winston 500. Some fans say Elliott's drive to victory that day was the most sensational effort in NASCAR history. Awesome Bill made up two full laps – more than five miles at Talladega – all under green-flag conditions to win his second of the Winston Million events and a chance to collect a million dollars at Darlington.

That's pretty heady stuff for a young man from the North Georgia mountains, but Elliott, all things considered, handled it pretty well. Two South Carolina highway patrolmen were assigned to Elliott. Every newspaper, every radio station, every television station, every magazine, every talk show – you name it, they all wanted a word with the stock car driver who could win a million dollars in the Southern 500 at Darlington.

Never before in history had so many eyes and ears been focused on a town of 5,000 in a state with no other professional sports. Darlington and Bill Elliott were the talk of America.

Elliott captured the pole position in qualifying, which heightened the interest in his Winston Million quest. And, the race lived up to its billing.

Elliott led the first 14 laps before Dale Earnhardt streaked past. He concentrated on racing the track, but found himself back out front after 63 laps, where he remained until Harry Gant took the lead for a time.

"I was just trying to stay out of the wall," said Elliott. "There was a lot of pressure on, and I sure didn't want to make a mistake."

In the closing stages of the race, Cale Yarborough, win-

(Left) Harry Gant (right) and team owner (Hollywood stuntman) Hal Needham raise the 1984 Southern 500 trophy.

(Below) A young Bobby Hillin takes tires and fuel on a pit stop during the '85 Southern 500.

A young Bill Elliott, shown here in 1981 with legendary mechanic–crew chief "Suitacse Jake" Elder (left) went on to win five NASCAR Winston Cup Series races at Darlington – including the '85 Southern 500, and with it, the Winston Million.

Bill Elliott's Winston Million – winning Thunderbird is on display at Darlington's NMPA Stock Car Hall of Fame Joe Weatherly Museum.

(Inset) Bill Elliott is interviewed by ESPN's Dr. Dick Berggren after winning the '85 Southern 500 and the Winston Million bonus.

DARLINGTON
Winston Million
Bill Elliott
$1,000,000
ONE MILLION DOLLARS
Winston Cigarettes

76
UNOCAL
GOODYEAR
PEAK
Winston
STP
CHAMPION
BUSCH
MOOG
MICHIGAN
Goody's
Holley
Edelbrock
9
EAGLE
CRANE cams
Gatorade
MOROSO
STP

ner of five Southern 500's, had the lead with Elliott riding his slipstream, waiting for an opportunity to pass. That opportunity came on lap 324, when a huge plume of smoke came from underneath Cale's car as they raced out of the fourth turn.

Elliott dove to the bottom of the track as Cale checked up and headed for pit road, where his crew discovered he had blown a power steering line. When Yarborough came out of the pits, he made a valiant effort to run down Elliott, but Awesome Bill was destined to become "Million Dollar Bill" on this exciting Darlington day.

The packed house went wild. Victory lane was strewn with fake million dollar bills bearing Elliott's picture on them. It was a happy, happy scene and a great moment for all of NASCAR.

Elliott's prize money for the day was a whopping $1,053,725 – by far the most money a NASCAR driver had ever earned in one race.

Leave it to Red Tyler to put things in perspective. "How in the dickens are we gonna ever top this?"

Bill Elliott had an answer: "I wouldn't mind doing it again next year . . . for the money part. I don't know whether I'd want to do all the other stuff, though."

While 1985 was Bill Elliott's year at Darlington, the tough, old track paid him

To date, Dale Earnhardt (pictured here in 1980) has won nine NASCAR Winston Cup Series races at Darlington, including the 1987 TranSouth 500 and Southern 500.

Tim Richmond (right) won the 1986 Southern 500. He's shown here in the early '80s, passing time with Neil Bonnett.

back the following year. Elliott was never a factor in the TranSouth 500. Neither, however, was anyone else except Dale Earnhardt. It was his time to shine, and the hard-driving Earnhardt routed the field. Earnhardt led all but 32 laps of the 367-lap event and was never passed on the track, finishing a full lap ahead of everyone except Darrell Waltrip, who finished second. Bobby Allison, Neil Bonnett and Tim Richmond rounded out the top five, but had been no match for Earnhardt at any time during the race.

Tim Richmond won the 1986 Southern 500 after a lengthy rain delay and after Bill Elliott slipped into Darlington's famous wall while leading with just six laps to go. Bobby Allison also passed Elliott for second place. Million-Dollar Bill wound up third, which paid a little over $25,000 – a far cry from the $1,053,725 he had won in the previous year's Southern 500.

The old race track wasn't through with Elliott. The very next year, Bill was in position to win the 1987 TranSouth 500, leading Dale Earnhardt as the two drivers started the final lap. But Elliott ran out of gas and Earnhardt won. Elliott finished second ahead of Richard Petty. Sterling Marlin was fourth and Ken Schrader fifth.

Young Mark Martin finished third – behind Gant and Darrell Waltrip – in the '83 TranSouth 500. To date, he's tasted victory once at Darlington, in the '93 Southern 500.

It was Earnhardt again on Labor Day weekend in the 1987 Southern 500. This time, Dale raced Richard Petty and the rain, beating them both. Earnhardt passed Petty just 12 laps before the bottom fell out and was declared the winner after the rain kept coming, preventing a restart. The race was 275.9 miles long – well over the halfway mark to make it official. Rusty Wallace finished second in one of his better Darlington performances. Petty was third, Sterling Marlin fourth and Terry Labonte finished fifth.

The 1988 TranSouth 500 turned into a battle of tires as Goodyear Tire and Rubber Company, "Goliath" in the race tire business, faced a challenge from Hoosier Tire, the "David" in racing tires. Persistent Bob Newton, president of the Hoosier race tire manufacturing company, was trying to compete on the NASCAR Winston Cup Series circuit against overwhelming odds.

Newton, an engineer, had successfully built and sold racing tires for years that were used in all types of short-track racing. It was Newton's dream to compete on the big tracks against Goodyear.

His presence in the NASCAR Winston Cup Series created quite a ripple, as teams had to choose which tires to use in each race. Many teams stuck with Goodyear, but several switched to Hoosier. The situation reminded old-timers of the days when Firestone and Goodyear battled it out for race-tire supremacy. The downside of such a tire war was the possibility of sacrificing reliability for speed. Many of the drivers, crew chiefs and car owners worried about where such a tire war would take them.

Nonetheless, Lake Speed, a former World Karting Association champion, drove his Hoosier-shod Oldsmobile to an upset victory at NASCAR's toughest track. It was considered an upset because it was the first time a car using Hoosier tires had won at Darlington, and it was also Lake Speed's first NASCAR Winston Cup Series win. Alan Kulwicki finished second, followed by Davey Allison, Bill Elliott and Sterling Marlin.

Speed was ecstatic following his first victory. "I've always dreamed of winning a race at this old place," he said, "and now I've done it. I'll never forget what Darel Dieringer (former Darlington winner and member of the National Motorsports Press Association Hall of Fame) told me about Darlington. "Darel told me I needed to see the place before I raced here for the first time. He drove me through the gate nearest the first turn, and I remember looking down the homestretch and thinking how narrow it looked. It looked like a drag strip. I still remember my first words as I was looking at that narrow straightaway. I said, 'You gotta be kidding!'"

The Hoosier-Goodyear tussle continued throughout the 1988 season, but Bill Elliott put Goodyear back in the Darlington winner's circle at the Southern 500. Elliott held off Rusty Wallace at the finish to capture his second Labor Day event, but this time around, there was no Winston Million waiting for him at the finish line.

The last year in the decade of the 80s produced a lot of headlines for Darlington Raceway. Red Tyler turned the day-to-day operation of the track over to Woodrow M. (Woody) McKay. "I'm headin' out to pasture," said the good-natured Tyler, who remained on the Board of Directors at the track as vice-chairman.

The Southern 500 is much more than just a race. The annual Southern 500 Parade is a highlight of each Labor Day weekend. Riding the Hall of Famers Float is (left to right) David Pearson, Ralph Moody, Raymond Parks, Jack Smith, Billy Watson (a friend of Parks), Ray Fox and Tim Flock.

Harry Gant won the TranSouth 500 in what turned out to be a cakewalk, if you can call surviving 367 laps around Darlington such a thing. Gant himself, a tough guy and one of the fittest drivers on the circuit, climbed out of his car looking as though he could run another 500 miles.

"I was confident we had the car to beat," said Harry. "I didn't want to tell anybody for fear it might jinx us, but I knew we'd win if we stayed out of trouble."

The rest of the top 10 read like a Who's Who of NASCAR. Gant finished one second ahead of up-and-coming Davey Allison, 20 years Gant's junior. Geoff Bodine finished third, Mark Martin fourth and Sterling Marlin took fifth place. Bill Elliott finished in sixth, Alan Kulwicki seventh, Rusty Wallace eighth, Michael Waltrip ninth and Lake Speed was 10th.

Prior to the 1989 Southern 500, Darlington officials announced a sponsor for the race, the first time in the history of Darlington that the classic event would be called anything other than the Southern 500. The race would now be known as the Heinz Southern 500. It was a natural fit. Race tracks and hot dogs go hand-in-hand, and Heinz ketchup would be the choice of all loyal NASCAR fans.

The upcoming Heinz Southern 500 had another driver eligible for the Winston Million bonus. Darrell Waltrip had started the season by winning the Daytona 500 and then grabbed the World 600 at Charlotte. Waltrip had won the TranSouth race at Darlington four times, but was still looking for his first Southern 500 victory.

The nicest thing to say about Waltrip's effort is, "It just wasn't Darrell's Day." Waltrip brushed the wall several times during the race and wound up 22nd, eight laps off the winning pace.

Dale Earnhardt won the race, held the day after his father, Ralph, was inducted into the NMPA Hall of Fame. It was Earnhardt's second Southern 500 win and nothing could have made Dale any happier than winning the race the day after his late father was recognized for his career in the sport. "Winning a million dollars wouldn't make me any happier than I was Saturday night. I'm so proud of my Dad, I can't describe it in words."

While the weekend was a wonderful experience for Earnhardt, Waltrip, in typical D.W. fashion, rattled off a little ditty to members of the media. "I love Darlington in the spring, and I love Darlington in the fall; I love Darlington in the winner's circle, but I hate Darlington in the wall!"

While most drivers light-heartedly compare Darlington Raceway's personality to that of the supernatural, Mother Nature herself took a huge swipe at the old track, as well as the entire coastal area of South Carolina a few weeks after the 1989 Southern 500.

Hurricane Hugo stormed into South Carolina, meandering inland with winds high enough to rip off part of the roof covering the Colvin grandstand and uprooting the supports for the Manufacturer's Box Seats along the backstretch.

The damage was significant enough to force the track to remove the roof altogether, and to pull down the box seat structure.

Darlington Raceway founder Harold Brasington stands in front of the turn-two grandstand which bears his name.

RANDSTAND

CHANGING WITH THE TIMES

What better way to usher in the 1990s at NASCAR's oldest superspeedway than to have "The Man," Dale Earnhardt, win both NASCAR Winston Cup Series races at the "Track Too Tough To Tame."

Earnhardt tamed it.

Driving Richard Childress' GM Goodwrench Chevrolet with reckless abandon, Earnhardt started the Darlington decade with domination. He drove the old track like he owned it. And, along with a few other NASCAR Hall of Famers like David Pearson, Bobby Allison, Buck Baker, Herb Thomas and Cale Yarborough, Earnhardt was fast becoming one of Darlington's biggest winners.

His wins in both the 1990 TranSouth 500 and the Southern 500 pushed his career win total at Darlington to seven, only a couple of victories behind all-time Darlington race winner Pearson. Racing writers began to tease Darlington General Manager Bill Kiser and Public Relations Director Russell Branham.

"When it comes to Earnhardt, your slogan doesn't fit," they said. "He's sure as heck tamed it!"

Earnhardt finished nearly a half-second ahead of Mark Martin in the TranSouth 500, with Davey Allison, Geoff Bodine and Morgan Shepherd rounding out the top five.

(Above) Team owner Richard Childress (left) and driver Dale Earnhardt (right) won both the TranSouth 500 and Heinz Southern 500 at Darlington in 1990. In all, Childress and Earnhardt have won at Darlington Raceway eight times together.

(Right) In 1987, Ken Schrader picked up his first NASCAR career pole position during qualifying for the TranSouth race. He, however, is still searching for his first career win at Darlington, but knows there's only one way to tame the 1.366-mile track.

How To Tame
DARLINGTON
* Go Fast
* Hope
* Turn left
* Hope
* Don't hit wall
* Hope

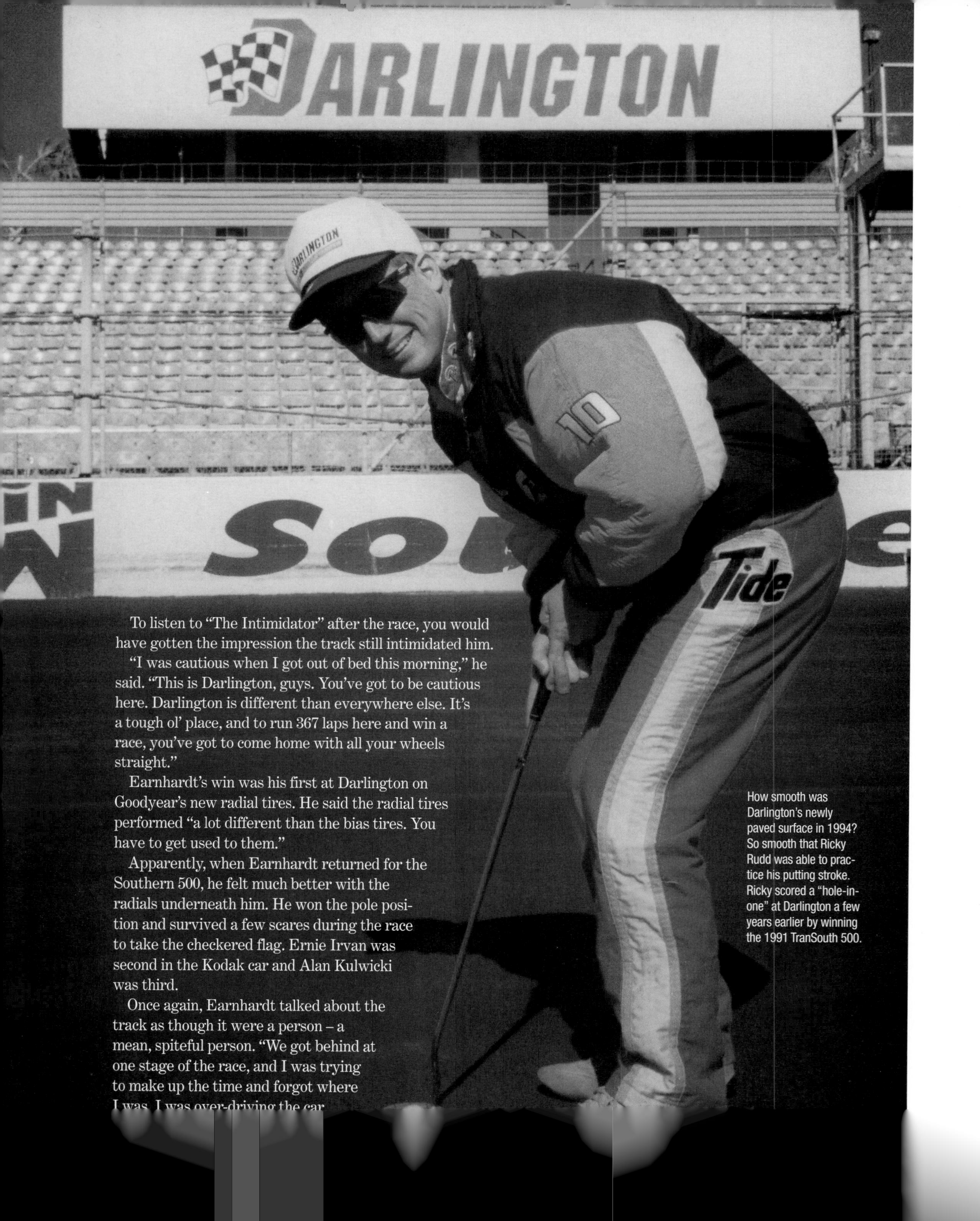

To listen to "The Intimidator" after the race, you would have gotten the impression the track still intimidated him.

"I was cautious when I got out of bed this morning," he said. "This is Darlington, guys. You've got to be cautious here. Darlington is different than everywhere else. It's a tough ol' place, and to run 367 laps here and win a race, you've got to come home with all your wheels straight."

Earnhardt's win was his first at Darlington on Goodyear's new radial tires. He said the radial tires performed "a lot different than the bias tires. You have to get used to them."

Apparently, when Earnhardt returned for the Southern 500, he felt much better with the radials underneath him. He won the pole position and survived a few scares during the race to take the checkered flag. Ernie Irvan was second in the Kodak car and Alan Kulwicki was third.

Once again, Earnhardt talked about the track as though it were a person – a mean, spiteful person. "We got behind at one stage of the race, and I was trying to make up the time and forgot where I was. I was over-driving the car

How smooth was Darlington's newly paved surface in 1994? So smooth that Ricky Rudd was able to practice his putting stroke. Ricky scored a "hole-in-one" at Darlington a few years earlier by winning the 1991 TranSouth 500.

"You saw the ol' gal jump up and slap me, didn't you? Put me right in the wall! Fortunately for us, I didn't hit the wall all that hard. We caught a caution flag and were able to put on new tires and pull the sheet metal back out where it's supposed to be.

"The ol' gal didn't knock me out. She just knocked me to my knees to remind me where I was. You can't ever forget that here. This is Darlington and you've got to remember that every lap, I mean every single lap."

Earnhardt grinned. "She was pretty good to us today, all things considered."

The Raceway itself was being spruced up by track President McKay, who divided his time between the track and his South Carolina House of Representatives duties. Flowers were planted, grass was mowed and a new garage for the visiting NASCAR Busch Series, Grand National Division cars had been built on the backstretch.

Track superintendent Sammy Yarborough, a cousin of Hall of Famer Cale Yarborough, treated the track grounds as though they were Middleton Gardens in Charleston or Brookgreen Gardens at Myrtle Beach. The place might be old, but it could be "neat-looking, respectable-looking," said Yarborough.

Thirty-five-year-old Ricky Rudd made it to Darlington's victory lane in the 1991 TranSouth 500 by "sticking to a good game plan. We ran consistent laps all day and my pit crew (headed by Waddell Wilson) got me in and out fast."

Rudd's Chevrolet crossed the finish line 11 seconds ahead of Davey Allison and just a few more car-lengths ahead of Michael Waltrip, who led the race on numerous occasions. Mark Martin was fourth and Rusty Wallace finished in fifth. Kyle Petty took sixth place, even though he "hates" the race track. ("Not the people in Darlington," says Kyle, "just the race track.") Ernie Irvan was seventh, Morgan Shepherd eighth, Geoff Bodine ninth and Sterling Marlin finished in 10th place.

The win was Rudd's first at Darlington and wound up being his only victory of the 1991 season, but the victory kept alive Rudd's streak of winning at least one race each season, dating back to 1983.

Lynda Petty was the Grand Marshal for the 42nd annual Southern 500. Darlington's Bill Kiser thought it fitting to honor Lynda for all the work she had done with the Winston Cup Racing Wives Auxiliary, an organization devoted to helping others.

Lynda's son Kyle made his return to the circuit in this event after being sidelined by surgery to repair a broken leg suffered in a crash at Talladega the previous May. Kyle ran strong in the race until an engine failure sent him to the sidelines.

Richard, the seven-time NASCAR Winston Cup Series champion, started well back in the field, but managed a respectable 16th-place finish, while another driver about the same age as The King covered the field again.

Ageless Harry Gant put in another flawless performance in his Leo Jackson Oldsmobile and beat Ernie Irvan, Ken Schrader, Derrick Cope, Terry Labonte and Sterling Marlin to the finish line. Gant, who qualified fifth, never led until the second half of the race. But, once the race reached the halfway point (183 laps), Gant charged to the front and led 152 of the remaining laps.

"We should have known we were in trouble right after qualifying," said one mechanic. "Gant's car was up on jack-stands Friday, and most of his team went to play golf. Harry didn't even come to the race track. That should have told us something right there."

Darlington Dominator: To date, Dale Earnhardt has won nine NASCAR Winston Cup Series races (second only to David Pearson, who won 10) and three NASCAR Busch Series events, at the Track Too Tough To Tame.

Bill Elliott, driving the Budweiser Ford owned by Junior Johnson, kept Harry Gant from winning back-to-back races at Darlington in the spring of 1992. Elliott put himself back in victory lane with a seven-second lead over Harry and Mark Martin.

It was one of the cleanest races in Darlington history with just four caution flags for 21 laps. Any of the top 20 finishers might have won the race, but the combination of Elliott behind the wheel and crew chief Tim Brewer in the pits proved to be too strong.

"Harry Gant's car was awful strong today, but my crew did such a good job, they kept getting me back on the track in position to win. There at the end, things just went our way," said Elliott, who chalked up his second TranSouth victory.

A review of the top 20 finishers for this event proves how much more important pit crews were becoming at the NASCAR Winston Cup Series level. Pickup pit crews who didn't practice and work on the little details that make pit stops quicker, were becoming more and more old-fashioned. The old adage "practice makes perfect" was beginning to pay off when a driver came in for a splash of gas and four new tires. One second lost in the pits could be the difference between winning and losing.

Bill Elliott has had a lot of reasons to smile at Darlington: He's won five times at the 1.366-mile oval, including the 1985 Southern 500, the first Winston Million race.

The 1992 NASCAR Winston Cup Series season was a pivotal year for the sport, and for Darlington Raceway. Things were changing fast. After all, there was a time when a 20-second pit stop was considered sensational. In 1992, a 20-second stop was considered slow. There was also a time when maybe five drivers were shoo-ins for victory if their cars made it to the finish of NASCAR's big races. Now, there were close to 25 drivers starting most races who had an honest-to-goodness chance to wind up in victory lane.

The pre-race focus in the garage area switched from who was going to win the race, to who was going to make the race. NASCAR developed provisional starting spots in an effort to help those teams who had supported the sport during its developmental years, but, with the number of talented drivers capable of winning races growing, everything was becoming more difficult.

It was, arguably, a much more competitive sport, if for no other reason, simply due to the numbers. Instead of just a few drivers having the financial support and the best equipment, a growing number of young drivers were finding opportunities to move to the NASCAR Winston Cup Series from NASCAR's grassroots divisions. Professional drivers from open-wheel (Midgets, Sprint Cars, Indycars) series were also being hired by car owners to participate in NASCAR's premier division.

The 1992 season was also the end of an era. The Richard Petty Fan Appreciation Tour heralded the end of King Richard's career as a driver. While Petty was climbing in and out of the cockpit for the last time at each NASCAR track on the circuit, he was being appropriately recognized for his contributions to the sport over the years.

Petty's final appearance as a driver at Darlington in the 1992 Southern 500 (where he started 31st and finished 20th) was totally overshadowed first, by Davey Allison's attempt to win the Winston Million, and finally, by Darrell Waltrip's first-time victory in a race he had been trying to win for 20 years.

"Ol' D.W." (as Darrell referred to himself), held the lead in the race at the end of 298 laps when a tremendous thunderstorm enveloped the track. Davey Allison, trying to become only the second driver ever to win the Winston Million (having qualified with victories in the Daytona 500 and the Winston 500 at Talladega), had pitted earlier than some (including Waltrip) and was running fifth when the race was stopped.

Mother Nature took over and the rain set in. Waltrip, having a little fun cutting-up for the television cameras during the delay, performed his own version of a rain dance in the pits. Finally, the race was called official as the rain continued with no letup in sight.

Waltrip was ecstatic. "I thought I was going to have a heart attack during that rain delay," he said. "I'm getting too old for that kind of drama. I still can't believe it. The

Good Lord just blessed us here today. I hate it for Davey, but you take 'em whenever you can get 'em, however you can get 'em."

Allison, displaying the demeanor that made him so popular with fans, expressed disappointment at the loss of his chance at a million-dollar payday, but maintained his sense of humor at the same time – a rarity in a pressure-packed situation such as his.

"The race car's still in one piece, so that's something considering this is Darlington. We know we did our best. I didn't hit the wall and that's pretty easy to do here. There's nothing we could do to change the weather. And, there's nothing we could have done to change the other teams' strategies, so I just look at it like, 'that's the way it goes.'"

Ironically, Darrell was not the first Waltrip to win at Darlington on this particular weekend. His younger brother, Michael, won the NASCAR Busch Series, Grand National Division race the day before. Michael was an emerging star in NASCAR, as was another youngster in that weekend's NASCAR Busch Series race, Jeff Gordon, who had driven a Baby Ruth-sponsored car for a couple of seasons in that series. Gordon had burst onto the NASCAR scene with a long history of success in open-wheel competition, although he

Michael Waltrip tries out a new hat? Actually, it's his trophy after winning the 1983 Daytona Dash Series race at Darlington. He scored another Darlington victory in 1992 when he won the Gatorade 200 NASCAR Busch Series event.

Goodwrench
3
LUMINA
SIMPSON
3
6

Nine-time Darlington winner Dale Earnhardt (#3) is being pursued by the quartet of Sterling Marlin (#4), Mark Martin (#6), Hut Stricklin (#26) and Rusty Wallace (#2) in the 1993 Southern 500.

In 1996, nine-time NASCAR Winston Cup Series winner at Darlington Dale Earnhardt was featured on the track's special "Legends of Darlington" pole day collectible ticket. Mac Josey, the track's Director of Ticket Operations, presented Earnhardt with a replica.

didn't look old enough to have a driver's license.

By age five, Jeff was driving go-karts and Quarter-Midgets, and won his first Quarter-Midget national championship just three years later. At age nine, he won the national Quarter-Midget title for the second consecutive year. Gordon's second quarter-midget title came in the same year (1980) his eventual Rick Hendrick teammate, Terry Labonte, won Darlington's Southern 500 at the ripe old age of 24.

Championships came easily for Gordon. In 1990, he captured the USAC Midget championship, then won the USAC Silver Crown title the following year. Gordon also won the NASCAR Busch Series Rookie of the Year title in 1991. In 1992, he won three NASCAR Busch Series races and 11 poles.

In 1993, the first year Gordon came to Darlington as a full-fledged NASCAR Winston Cup Series rookie, the Raceway was undergoing several changes. Jim Hunter came to Darlington and Woody McKay, the former President, was named Chairman of the Darlington Raceway Board.

Track General Manager Bill Kiser retired after receiving the state's highest honor – the Order of the Palmetto – from then-Governor Carroll Campbell. Kiser had served the old track well for more than two decades and was perhaps one of the sport's best-known, and well-liked men within the NASCAR garage and media circles.

Ironically, Gordon's first NASCAR Winston Cup Series appearance at Darlington was cut short. He ran only 275 of the 367 laps in the 1993 TranSouth Financial 500, before pulling into the garage with an ill-handling race car following a collision with a lapped car.

Gordon was one of three Rookie of the Year contenders

in that race, the others being Bobby Labonte – the 1991 NASCAR Busch Series, Grand National Division champion – and Kenny Wallace, who had been runner-up to Bobby in the 1991 NASCAR Busch Series chase. (Kenny is one of three Wallace brothers in NASCAR racing.) Labonte was the highest-finishing rookie in the race with an 18th-place showing. Gordon, however, wound up winning the NASCAR Winston Cup Series Rookie of the Year title.

Dale Earnhardt continued his winning ways at Darlington, taking the checkered flag at the old track for the fifth time in the spring race and the eighth time in his career. (Earnhardt had won the Southern 500 three times.)

The fifth time was the charm for Earnhardt. Time trials were rained out and the starting lineup for the race was determined by point standings, which put Earnhardt in the top spot. The big question in everyone's mind before qualifying was, "Can anyone break the 30-second barrier at Darlington?" Earnhardt himself had broken it unofficially during practice with a lap at 29.95 seconds. (The track qualifying record was held at the time by Sterling Marlin: 30.15 seconds at 163.067 mph).

When you stop and think about Marlin's lap speed, it is an amazing statistic. Remember: The fastest qualifying speed for the first race at Darlington back in 1950 was 82.350 miles per hour, set by Wally Campbell in an Oldsmobile.

On basically the same old track – same width, same tough old turns with a fraction more banking – speeds had doubled in 40 years, prompting the always-witty Buddy Baker to quip, "The turns at Darlington look about as big as that teeny little hole in a sewing needle. Every time you get to the end of the straightaway, you take a deep breath

Jeff Gordon looked a little different when he burst onto the NASCAR Winston Cup Series scene, sporting a mustache, alongside his publicist Ron Miller in 1993.

and hold it 'til you come out on the other side."

Buddy's father, Buck, put it another way: "Every time you go into one of those turns at Darlington, no matter how many years you've been racing there, your mind flashes the same old message to you. Man, there's gonna be a helluva wreck if I don't put on the brakes! If a driver let his mind take over, he'd come out of the race with a broken jaw. His foot would fly off that accelerator so fast, his knee would come up and break his jaw!"

Earnhardt's win was the 54th of his career and his average speed set a new record for the 500-mile distance at Darlington: 139.958 mph. He was almost two seconds ahead of runner-up Mark Martin and third-place finisher Dale Jarrett. Ken Schrader was fourth and Alan Kulwicki finished fifth.

"He loves this track and it shows," said Kulwicki, the 1992 NASCAR Winston Cup Series champion, of Earnhardt's victory. "You've got to run this place smart. Earnhardt does that as well or better than anyone else. You have to do your best with what you have and take the race as it goes. Today, it was Earnhardt's. Maybe there will come a day when we'll be better here."

Kulwicki had been one of the NASCAR drivers in the first International Race of Champions (IROC) events at Darlington, but mechanical problems forced him to the sidelines.

Davey Allison went on to beat NASCAR stars Dale Earnhardt, Harry Gant, Rusty Wallace and Ricky Rudd, as well as international star Juan Fangio, road racing stars Davy Jones and Jack Baldwin, and former Indianapolis 500 winner Al Unser Sr. In the end, the international and road racing stars could not keep up with the NASCAR guys.

Now, by no means is such a statement meant to belittle the abilities of road racers as compared to the NASCAR drivers. There have been many exciting battles on the flat-out tracks such as Daytona, Michigan and Talladega, where road racers like Jack Baldwin and Al Unser Jr., have held their own with the NASCAR boys. But, Darlington is just "Too Tough To Tame" for someone unaccustomed to the track's peculiarities.

Tragedy struck the sport in the springtime and again in early summer of 1993. Defending NASCAR Winston Cup Series Champion Alan Kulwicki died in a plane crash on his way to Bristol, and Davey Allison – winner of 17 NASCAR Winston Cup Series events and one of the most popular young drivers in the history of NASCAR – was killed

Mark Martin has been a dominant driver in NASCAR Busch Series races at the 1.366-mile oval, winning a record five events. He also picked up a victory in the 1993 Southern 500.

PEPSI
U
MOUNTAIN DEW
V
400
WINN DIXIE
60
THUNDERBIRD
60
Winston

in July when a helicopter he was flying crashed while landing at Talladega Superspeedway.

The 1993 Southern 500 was cut short by darkness after rain forced officials to delay the start by more than two hours, but Mark Martin (who had won three races in a row) won his fourth consecutive race when he took the checkered flag nearly two seconds ahead of Brett Bodine. It was Martin's first NASCAR Winston Cup Series win at Darlington and it was Bodine's best finish at the track. Rusty Wallace, Dale Earnhardt and Ernie Irvan rounded out the top five finishers.

It was Irvan's first race in the Ford formerly driven by Davey Allison. Earnhardt went on to win his record-tying (with Richard Petty) seventh NASCAR Winston Cup Series title. In the Rookie of the Year battle, Kenny Wallace wound up with the best finish (10th) while Bobby Labonte was 14th and Gordon 22nd.

Martin's win came as no surprise since many of the favored drivers mentioned Mark in a pre-race poll as the one racer other than themselves they would pick to win. Included among those giving Martin the nod were Earnhardt ("Mark's on a roll right now," said Dale), Earnhardt's car owner Richard Childress, former Southern 500 winner Darrell Waltrip, Kodak team owner Larry McClure and Chevrolet driver Dale Jarrett. Their reason for choosing Martin to win might have come as a result of his winning the Saturday Gatorade 200 for NASCAR Busch Series cars.

Two guys who love to race at Darlington – Jeff Gordon (left) and Mark Martin. Martin won the 1993 Southern 500, a race that started late due to rain and ended early because of darkness. Gordon has five Darlington victories to his credit, including four consecutive Pepsi Southern 500s.

Just days before the massive new grandstand bearing his name was completed (Tyler Tower), former Raceway President Walter D. (Red) Tyler passed away. Just a few days before his death, Tyler helped serve construction workers box lunches as they worked around the clock to get his namesake finished in time for the 1994 TranSouth Financial 400.

And, as would be expected, he had some fun at his own expense. "I don't want no grandstand named after me. I know how these things work. You can't put somebody's name on anything in racing without it costing something. I keep asking what it's gonna cost and they keep telling me, 'Red, don't worry about it!'"

Tyler's services were attended by virtually

everyone who was anyone in NASCAR racing, and, if they didn't attend, they sent expressions of sympathy to the family, or Tyler's beloved track.

Even fans who didn't know Tyler personally but knew of his racing personality through trade publications, called the track to express their condolences. Tyler was like a father figure to me (as well as a good friend for many years) and would have reacted to all those calls with something like, "Did you sell them a ticket to the TranSouth Financial 400?"

Dale Earnhardt spoke for the entire racing community regarding Tyler's passing when he said, "Red was a heckuva man. He was a real racer. Things won't be the same at Darlington without him."

During pre-race ceremonies for the 1994 TranSouth Financial 400, the new Tyler Tower grandstand was officially dedicated in Red's memory, and one of his favorite race drivers, Dale Earnhardt, another "real racer," won the race.

It was Earnhardt's ninth career win at the egg-shaped track and runner-up Mark Martin left no doubt in anyone's mind about just how good Earnhardt was on this particular Sunday.

"Man, Earnhardt just wore us out," Martin explained afterwards. "From the first lap to the last one, we ran our guts out. He just wore us out."

Bill Elliott finished third after setting a new Darlington qualifying record in his Budweiser-sponsored Ford at 29.704 seconds (165.553 mph), beating the old mark set by Sterling Marlin for the 1992 TranSouth 500 (30.157 seconds at 163.067 mph.) Rounding out the top 10 were Dale Jarrett, Lake Speed, Ernie Irvan, Ken Schrader, Harry Gant, Ricky Rudd and Ted Musgrave.

Darlington's best. Dale Earnhardt (right), with nine wins, credits all-time Darlington winner David Pearson with much of his success at the track "Too Tough To Tame." Pearson once drove for an injured Earnhardt at Darlington, and won the race.

Earnhardt's accomplishment on this particular race day was awesome, considering the surface on the old track "chewed up" tires after 20 laps or so.

"Today was one of those deals where, if you didn't pace yourself and run the race you wanted to run, you'd use your tires up real quick," said Earnhardt. "This old track is still too tough to tame. She's rough, the surface is abrasive and she's mean. We just respected her all day and she wound up being good to us."

Earnhardt dedicated the win to his good buddy, Neil

These two know of only one way to drive Darlington – wide open! That's Jimmy Spencer (#23) and Dick Trickle in the Ford of South Carolina's own Bud Moore.

15
DICK TRICKLE
Ford
QualityCare
15
FORD
LINCOLN
MERCURY
GOODYEAR
Winston Cup
Holley
SIMPSON
MOOG
CRAFTSMAN
CRAFTSMAN

Bonnett (winner of the 1981 Southern 500), who died in a crash during practice at Daytona International Speedway earlier in the year. "I'm thinking about his wife, Susan, and his whole family. I miss Neil tremendously. We fished and hunted and hung out together, and I miss him more every day. Darlington reminds me of Neil because he loved to race here."

Earnhardt's ninth Darlington win put him within one victory of tying David Pearson's all-time Darlington career record of 10 wins. (Actually, Pearson won 11 races at Darlington, counting his Late Model Sportsman win in the 1980 TranSouth 200.) Ironically, one of Pearson's wins, the 1979 TranSouth 500, came as a result of Pearson filling in for Earnhardt, who had suffered a broken shoulder and was unable to compete at Darlington in that event. It was the only race Earnhardt missed during his entire career.

Earnhardt said his success at Darlington, in some measure, was largely due to the help he received as a young driver from the veteran Pearson. "I remember exactly the words of advice Pearson gave me when I was a rookie at Darlington," said Earnhardt, twisting his face into a huge grin. "He said, 'Get out of my way!' That's exactly what he said!"

Dale chuckled and added, "Seriously, David helped me some. He talked to me about cars and how to drive them. I watched David race against my Dad and he was a great competitor and used his head a lot."

Bobby Allison, a five-time Darlington winner himself (including four Southern 500s), says any similarities in driving styles between Pearson and Earnhardt are "more on the mental side of things. Both of them focus on the checkered flag. The way they get there is not all that similar. Pearson was the most patient guy I've ever seen in a race car. He knew

(Above) From one top cat to another. Darlington's all-time pole winner, David Pearson, presents Jeff Gordon with Darlington's Polecat trophy for the 1995 TranSouth Financial 400 top starting position.

(Right) Sterling Marlin lived his dream of winning at Darlington by taking the checkered flag for the 1995 TranSouth Financial 400. In victory lane (inset), Sterling expresses the true joy of victory.

Kodak
Film
SIMPSON
Kodak
Delco
FILM
76
film
Delco Battery
MONTE CARLO

when to wait and when to just let the other guys do themselves in. That way, he didn't have to race them.

"Earnhardt races everybody from the green flag on. But he's got a feel for where he is and what he needs to do. Earnhardt has the ability to adapt his driving style to the track, especially Darlington, as it changes. And everybody knows, Darlington changes just about every lap you run there.

"To win at Darlington, you've got to be both aggressive and patient. You have to know when to go, and when to wait. Earnhardt has been very good at that over the years, but his style, overall, is to be more aggressive. No one would say it hasn't worked well for him, would they?"

While Mark Martin finished behind Earnhardt in the 1994 TranSouth 400, he finished ahead of him in the IROC race. Rusty Wallace was second, and road racer Jack Baldwin finished third. Earnhardt finished fourth and Kyle Petty was fifth, followed by Scott Sharp, Tom Kendall, Geoff Brabham, Danny Sullivan, Al Unser Jr., Steve Kinser and Dale Jarrett. Jarrett and Kinser were eliminated in a crash on the ninth circuit of the 46-lap event.

Two of the biggest names in NASCAR racing were in the limelight during 1994 Labor Day weekend festivities. Bill Elliott won his third Mountain Dew Southern 500, finishing six seconds ahead of Dale Earnhardt's Chevrolet. It had been nine years since "Awesome Bill from Dawsonville" became "Million-Dollar Bill" at Darlington with his huge win in the inaugural year of the Winston Million bonus program.

Rounding out the top 10 were Morgan Shepherd, Ricky Rudd, Sterling Marlin, Jeff Gordon (this was the first time Gordon finished in the top 10 at Darlington), Rusty Wallace, Jeff Burton (this was also the first time Burton finished in the top 10 at Darlington), Dale Jarrett and Terry Labonte.

John Andretti was the "Top Cat" in 1995, capturing his first career NASCAR pole position for the Southern 500, in only his third appearance at the track.

This particular Labor Day weekend was also special for Cale Yarborough, as the South Carolinian was inducted into the National Motorsports Press Association Hall of Fame. The induction ceremonies were held in Darlington's J.C. Daniels Auditorium, just a few yards off the site of Cale's first-ever racing victory.

"I won my first race right there on Darlington's North Main Street, a Soap Box Derby," said Cale during his induction.

The "old lady" of racing, Darlington Raceway, received a full facelift over the winter of 1994. Former Indianapolis Motor Speedway superintendent Clarence Cagle came to Darlington to oversee a complete repaving of the track.

When the 1995 TranSouth Financial 400 weekend rolled around, the track surface was brand-new and many of the drivers who had tested during the winter after the asphalt had time to cure, said the resurfacing was going to make Darlington Raceway even tougher than before, because they'd be able to get a grip for passing in the corners.

What the new track surface actually did was increase twice as fast as they had run when the track opened in 1950. If you had told someone back in 1950 that stock cars would someday run speeds over 170 miles per hour, they would have thought you were just as crazy as Harold Brasington for building the track in the first place.

This race produced another first-time Darlington winner, Sterling Marlin of Columbia, Tenn., another second-generation driver in the NASCAR Winston Cup Series ranks. Marlin took the checkered flag by little more than one second over Dale Earnhardt. Ted Musgrave, an up-and-coming young driver from the Midwest with a long string

Jeff Gordon was greeted by Miss Southern 500, Janet Powers, after his 1996 Southern 500 victory. The next year, Janet won the title of Miss South Carolina, representing Darlington Raceway as Miss Southern 500. This was the second of four consecutive Southern 500 crowns for Gordon.

speeds. Jeff Gordon won the pole position during first-round qualifying. (At Darlington, the Busch Pole Award winner receives the "Polecat Trophy," designed by award-winning artist-sculptor Patz Fowle of Hartsville, S.C., who also created the life-size version of Darlington's "Race-a-saurus Wrecks," which is on permanent display in the Myrtle Beach NASCAR Café).

Gordon literally shattered the old record, trimming nearly a full second off the old mark of 29.704 seconds (165.553 mph) with a run of 28.786 seconds at an incredible speed of 170.833 mph. The cars were now racing well over

of short-track victories, finished third (his best finish in a NASCAR Winston Cup Series race to date). Another young driver with strong family ties in the sport, Todd Bodine (younger brother of both Geoff and Brett), finished fourth, and former Daytona 500 winner Derrick Cope wound up fifth.

Gordon led during the early and middle stages of the

After claiming his first career NASCAR pole for the 1995 Southern 500, John Andretti (#37) shows the way for former Darlington winner Lake Speed (1988 TranSouth Financial 400) and Geoff Bodine (#7).

9
SPAM
9
MELLING
OIL PUMPS
EXIDE
BATTERIES
EXIDE
7
THUNDERBIRD

Cup Series
DARLINGTON
A NASCAR TRADITION
THE "NEW"
START/FINISH
LINE
KODI

race, but was eliminated in an accident after he had completed 200 of the 293-lap distance.

Marlin was appreciative of the track's history and tradition after winning his first race at the fabled old place he came to as a kid with his racing father.

"I used to come over here with my dad," he said, "and usually, I'd drive the truck over for him."

Sterling's father, "Coo Coo" (real name: Clifton), was one of NASCAR's front-running independents.

"My dad didn't like Darlington all that much. I remember the first time I drove here, I was a little faster than he was and that made him mad. But I've always enjoyed Darlington. This is a neat old place. It's a tough old place, no doubt about that. Everything just went my way today." Marlin added, "Look, any time you beat Dale Earnhardt, anytime, any place, it's great. Dale is certainly one of the best drivers out there and he runs this place awfully well, too, so my hat's off to the entire Kodak crew for getting me into victory lane at Darlington."

Mark Martin won the final IROC race at Darlington, followed by Jeff Gordon, Ken Schrader and road racers Tom Kendall and Scott Pruett.

A beautiful young woman from Spartanburg, S.C., put Darlington Raceway back in the news during the summer of 1995. Amanda Spivey, the reigning Miss Southern 500, won the prestigious Miss South Carolina Pageant to become the first Miss Southern 500 to win the South Carolina title since the inception of the Miss Southern 500 Pageant in 1953.

One of the most famous names in motorsports grabbed the pole position for the 1995 Southern 500. John Andretti, nephew of Indianapolis 500 winner Mario and cousin of CART star Michael, drove his Ford to the fastest time in only his third appearance at Darlington Raceway and couldn't believe he had done it.

"I certainly wanted to win a pole position," said Andretti, "but I never expected it to come at a place like Darlington. To get my first one here is really special."

Andretti kept his Ford in front, or near the front, for the first 100 laps, but old "Mr. Darlington" himself, Dale Earnhardt, dominated the middle portions of the event. As the race played out, the brightly-colored DuPont Chevrolet of young Jeff Gordon moved up through the field. Gordon had been running in the top 10 throughout the afternoon and took the lead shortly after 280 laps were completed. Down the stretch in the 367-lap dash, Ricky Rudd, Andretti and Rusty Wallace took turns leading, but Gordon

The historic "switching" of the start/finish line came about in 1997, and drivers Steve Grissom and Mike Skinner showed their hand at painting the new line.

After Grissom and Skinner painted the new stripe, the ribbon-cutting ceremony took place. Participating in the festivities were (left to right) Darlington Raceway President Jim Hunter, South Carolina Governor David Beasley, First Lady Mary Wood Beasley, South Carolina Senator Strom Thurmond (who was part of the inaugural ribbon-cutting in 1950) and NASCAR President Bill France Jr.

came to the front 35 laps from the finish and stayed there for his first Darlington victory. Dale Earnhardt added another runner-up finish to his collection, with Wallace third, newcomer Ward Burton fourth and Michael Waltrip fifth. Andretti wound up 11th after a late-race stop cost him valuable track position.

Gordon's first Darlington victory came in his sixth start, and it was the 25-year-old's sixth win of the 1995 season. He was extremely excited afterwards.

"Any time you come out of a race here with your car in one piece, you're lucky. To come out of here with a win is just unbelievable. This is a tough race track just to finish a race, much less win a race. The car was just awesome today, and the crew did everything they needed to do to keep me in contention."

While the 1995 Labor Day weekend will be remembered as the first year Jeff Gordon won the Southern 500, it will also be remembered as the weekend Jack Roush announced the hiring of Jeff Burton, NASCAR's 1994 Winston Cup Series Rookie of the Year, to drive for his new Exide-sponsored Ford team in 1996.

Gordon, who went on to win his first NASCAR Winston Cup Series championship in 1995, returned to Darlington to win both the TranSouth Financial 400 and the Mountain Dew Southern 500 in 1996. Dale Jarrett had a shot at the Winston Million, but scraped the wall early in the race and was never a threat after that. Hut Stricklin had his best career finish, trailing Gordon across the line in second.

Raceway officials announced an additional tower grandstand for 1997, to be named after all-time Darlington winner David Pearson. It would be called the Pearson Tower. Dale Jarrett fared much better than he did in his Winston Million bid the next time around. Jarrett held off a late-race charge by Ted Musgrave to make his first appearance in Darlington's victory lane for a NASCAR Winston Cup Series win. (Jarrett had visited victory lane twice before in NASCAR Busch Series races, winning the 1990 Gatorade 200 and the 1991 Pontiac 200.)

Jarrett's victory was very popular with fans. He had been coming to Darlington since he was a young boy to watch his father, Ned, race. "I can remember when my dad won the Southern 500 and how exciting it was. I said to myself, 'One of these days when I grow up, I'm gonna win the Southern 500.' This might not be the Southern 500, but it's Darlington."

Jarrett had started the 1996 season by winning the Daytona 500. CBS, with Dale's father in the broadcast booth, captured one of the most poignant moments in sports history. The director asked Ned Jarrett to call the last laps of the race as his son roared toward the finish line with Dale Earnhardt in dogged pursuit.

"He's gonna win it! He's gonna win it! Dale Jarrett is gonna win the Daytona 500!" Ned couldn't hide his emotions or his enthusiasm, and rightly so.

Dale, a popular figure in the Darlington area, told Darlington PR Director Russell Branham he would attend a morning kickoff to a Darlington County Scholarship Program two days after the Daytona 500.

On Monday, Branham began frantically trying to get in touch with Jarrett. Jarrett didn't return Branham's calls. Monday afternoon, Branham started making backup plans in case Jarrett canceled out.

At 8:00 a.m. Tuesday morning, Jarrett drove up in front of Darlington's St. John's High School. Branham was relieved.

"Hey, Russell! I told you I'd be here, didn't I? But I

Prior to running for the Winston Million in 1996, Dale Jarrett was presented a special award for his contributions to the Palmetto State by Grace McCown (left), director of South Carolina Parks, Recreation and Tourism, and Darlington Raceway President Jim Hunter (right). Jarrett, who lived in nearby Camden, S.C., for a few years as a child, came up short in his bid to claim the $1 million bonus.

ought to bop you on the head," joked Jarrett. "I had to get up at 4:30 this morning to get here in time. You owe me, buddy, big-time."

During his articulate presentation to the high school students that morning, Jarrett told the story about what his daughter had said when she went to school the day after his Daytona 500 victory and was asked by the teacher, "Well, did anything exciting happen to you over the weekend that you'd like to tell us about?"

Jarrett said his young daughter never missed a beat and quickly replied, "Oh yes! I got to go to Disney World!"

"I don't guess my Daytona 500 win stood very high on her list of priorities," said Dale with a laugh.

Jarrett's appearance at that scholarship announcement stuck in the minds of the Raceway staff. So, his victory in the following year's (1997) TranSouth 400 prompted a steady stream of Raceway personnel to victory lane before the ceremonies ended.

Jarrett's crew chief, Todd Parrott, a second-generation NASCAR crew chief (his father, Buddy Parrott, has been crew chief for many of NASCAR's most talented drivers, including Jeff Burton) lauded his Ford Quality Care team.

"I can't say enough about this team. And what about that race car driver? That son-of-a-gun is awesome! We finally won at Darlington!"

Jarrett was just as excited.

Dale Jarrett notched his first career Darlington pole for the 1996 Southern 500 and led the field at the drop of the green flag. Outside pole-sitter Jeff Gordon went on to win the event. Honorary Starter Janine Bousquette waves the green flag.

"That finish was too exciting! I really didn't think I could hold Ted (Musgrave) off. I know he was after that first victory, and I cut him off and didn't give him any racing room a lot of times in the last 10 laps. He would have been justified to hit me harder than he did coming off that last corner.

"To win at Darlington was a special feeling. I've won here in a Busch car, but to win a Winston Cup race here, that's an accomplishment. It ranks right near the top. Dad just said, 'Congratulations!' But he realizes how difficult it is to win here and what winning here means to a driver. It puts a notch in your belt when you win here. This is the toughest place, by far, that we race."

Runner-up Musgrave said his and Jarrett's cars "were pushing like two dump trucks there at the end. I nerfed him a little bit and turned him sideways a little bit. But you just rough folks up as much as you can, but still be clean about it because I know it's gonna be my turn one of these days.

"We touched and we bumped and we did everything we could possibly do to win. I could have taken him out but that's not our style of racing. There will be a day when Dale Jarrett will be on my bumper and he will return the favor."

Raceway officials switched the start/finish line to the south side of the track from the north side prior to the 1997 Mountain Dew

When the new tower overlooking turn four was being built in 1997, the name choice was an obvious one: Pearson Tower, named after Darlington's all-time winner, David Pearson (left), joined here by track President Jim Hunter.

Southern 500, in order to accommodate expansion plans for more seats and additional spectator parking. The switch obviously didn't have any affect on Jeff Gordon's mastery of the Darlington track as he won the race for the second consecutive time.

At the same time, he became the second driver to win the Winston Million, beating Jeff Burton to the finish line after they swapped sparks on the final lap. It was certainly a hair-raising finish.

"I'm blown away," said Gordon. "Yeah, I blocked him when he (Burton) tried to pass. He hit me in the right-rear bumper and I'm just glad I didn't spin. I'm sure he's not happy, but man, I'm going for a million dollars. I said all week if it came down to that, I'd have to go for it! Ray (Evernham, Gordon's crew chief) kept telling me, 'You can do it! You can do it!' Man, he didn't know how bad that car was pushing. We raced hard. Yeah, we slammed and banged. It was a great race, though."

Burton was tired and disappointed.

"Gordon was racing for a million dollars. I got under him on the last lap and when he cut down on me. I'll be honest. I turned right on him. I just didn't get him good enough. I thought Dale (Jarrett, who finished third) was going to win the race because I was gonna do my best to make sure he (Gordon) didn't win the race when he cut down on me.

"I'm not saying I wouldn't do the same thing for a million dollars. You can't blame the guy. But we're here to win, too. He won the race, what can you say? He did what he had to do to win the race."

Dale Earnhardt scared everyone at the start of the race when he grazed the wall, weaving erratically around the track for a couple of laps before finally pulling back into the pits after the race was underway. Earnhardt was taken to a local hospital where doctors ran every test possible to discover why he became dizzy and finally passed out after managing to get his race car back into the pits. He was released from the hospital the following morning, had his own doctors run additional tests and showed up at Richmond the following weekend ready to race. It became known as the "phantom knockout" and everyone who knows The Intimidator agreed it was the only way you could knock a tough customer like Earnhardt out and live to tell about it.

Earnhardt was relieved by NASCAR Busch Series driver Mike Dillon, who finished 30th. Trailing Gordon, Burton and Jarrett across the finish line on Gordon's million-dollar day were Bill Elliott, Ricky Rudd, Terry Labonte, Bobby Labonte (who had started from the pole position), Mark Martin, Michael Waltrip and Ken Schrader.

Many of the drivers in the 1997 Southern 500 attended induction ceremonies for three new members of the National Motorsports Press Association Hall of Fame the night before the race. Inducted were Buddy Baker, who joined his father, Buck, as an inductee, Jack Ingram, known as "Iron Man" for his tenacity as a NASCAR Busch Series champion, and everyone's favorite, the late Neil Bonnett.

Janet Powers – 1997 Miss Southern 500 – won the Miss South Carolina title, prompting a huge "Welcome Home" celebration. Janet grew up in Hartsville, S.C., just down

Ah, the thrill of a $1 million victory. That's Jeff Gordon in 1998 after winning the Pepsi Southern 500 and capturing Winston's No Bull 5 bonus.

INTERSTATE BATTERIES
Coca-Cola
WIX
SIMPSON
MBNA
INTERSTATE BATTERIES
CIRCUIT CITY
GUMOUT
BATTERIES

Darlington Raceway, home of the infamous "Darlington Stripe." Stock car drivers have left more paint on her concrete walls than the track crew. Here, Bobby Labonte recalls leaving some "Interstate Green" on the whitewashed fence.

The International Race of Champions (IROC) came to Darlington Raceway in 1993. The late Davey Allison outlasted the field to win the event. He was presented the winning trophy by Dan Cotter of True Value, and was joined in the winner's circle by his family.

the road from Darlington Raceway.

Dale Jarrett won the 1998 TranSouth Financial 400, ending Jeff Gordon's stranglehold on Darlington's victory lane, but Gordon came right back in the fall to win his fourth consecutive Pepsi Southern 500 and another million-dollar bonus from Winston that ultimately was lost in the shuffle of Gordon's overall success.

After all, this is a guy who had won nearly $10,000,000 in prize money after just six full years on the NASCAR Winston Cup Series circuit. That's not counting whatever he wins in 1999 or beyond, not to mention a mountain of product endorsements ranging from milk to Pepsi, souvenir collectibles worth millions, and being the hottest commodity in professional sports. In spite of all that, he's a real nice guy – as nice as someone can be when it seems that everyone in the world is trying to get a piece of your action.

He's still the same Jeff Gordon who charmed all the ladies at a fund-raising event in Darlington the first time he ever came to town as NASCAR Busch Series driver. He's still the same Jeff Gordon who loves to race. And, he's still – and, arguably, will always be – the best driver in NASCAR Winston Cup Series racing today.

A rain-shortened 1999 TranSouth Financial 400 produced one of the most bizarre finishes in Darlington Raceway history, and Jeff Burton became another first-time Darlington winner.

Burton was leading and was coming out of turn three when several cars tangled just off turn four. Cars slid in every direction down the front straightaway, and Burton's car hit the wall as he tried to steer through the wreckage, resulting in extensive damage to his car. Somehow, he managed to make it back to the start-finish line first to take the caution flag, then managed to nurse his crippled machine around the track for another lap before NASCAR officials red-flagged the race for a sudden thunderstorm. Jeremy Mayfield was second, Gordon third, Dale Jarrett fourth, Mark Martin fifth and rookie sensation Tony Stewart came home in sixth. Bobby Hamilton, Ward Burton, John Andretti and Bobby Labonte completed the top 10.

"I just saw the smoke and it got dark pretty quick and I might have just drove it into the wall," said Burton, who

(**Above**) Darlington Mayor Ronnie Ward (left) presented Jeff Burton with the winner's trophy after Burton was victorious in the 1997 Dura-Lube 200 NASCAR Busch Series race at Darlington. (**Below**) Not only has Darlington Raceway been a NASCAR tradition since 1950, but also an American tradition.

was the happiest man at the track when NASCAR called the race when it continued to rain. "We were either gonna win or finish dead last. There sure wasn't gonna be anything in between."

Whoever wins the 50th Anniversary running of the Pepsi Southern 500 at Darlington Raceway will certainly earn it. The winner will very likely be just like those who have preceded him: jubilant, to say the least. They'll know they've been in "one heckuva fight."

But even so, Darlington Raceway, NASCAR's crusty old curmudgeon of a race track, will give them something they can't get anywhere else on the NASCAR circuit. She'll give them "the feeling" – the Darlington feeling. The kind of deep-down feeling you carry with you for the rest of your life. She'll give you the feeling of winning. Really winning.

All the "real racers," as Dale Earnhardt calls them, know the feeling because they know if they can win at Darlington, they can win anywhere, anytime, anyplace.

And, in the end, that's what Darlington Raceway is all about, and has been for 50 years.

DARLINGTON MEMORIES

(Above) Clarice Lane, who has been part of the Raceway since its inception, joined Dale Earnhardt and his wife, Teresa, during the 1993 NASCAR Winston Cup Series Awards Banquet at the Waldorf Astoria Hotel in New York City. Clarice continues to work for the track today.

(Left) Paul Sawyer (left) current President of Richmond International Raceway and former Darlington Raceway President Bob Colvin (center), along with Richmond's Kenneth Campbell.

(Below Left) Darlington Raceway is proud to be part of South Carolina, home of Smiling Faces, Beautiful Places. Dale Earnhardt passes by the billboard, which is now located outside of turn four.

(Below) Darlington Raceway is glad to be a marketing partner with NASCAR Café in Myrtle Beach, S.C. The Raceway's Senior Advisor, Harold King (right), joined Dale Jarrett (center) and NASCAR Café President Mark Dyer at the Café in 1998 for a special charitable event.

(Above) The National Motorsports Press Association's Hall of Fame is located in the Joe Weatherly Museum on the grounds of Darlington Raceway. This duo won awards from the NMPA in 1993 – Darlington Raceway's Bridget Blackwell (the Joe Littlejohn Award for outstanding contributions to the NMPA) and The State newspaper's Jim McLaurin (The George Cunningham Award for being the outstanding writer).

(Below) Two NASCAR legends – former NASCAR Winston Cup Series Director Dick Beaty and former Darlington Raceway President Walter D. "Red" Tyler.

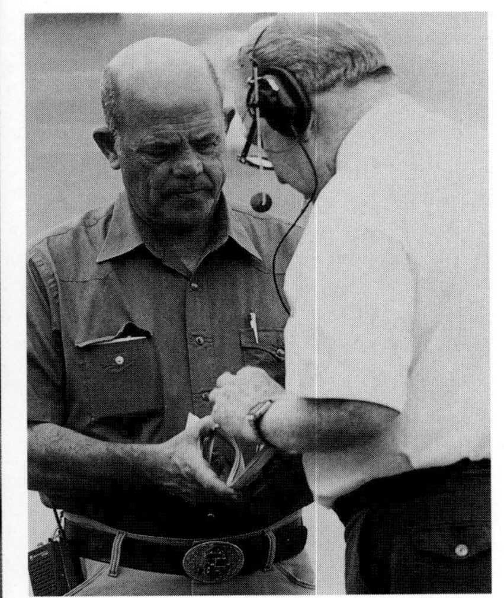

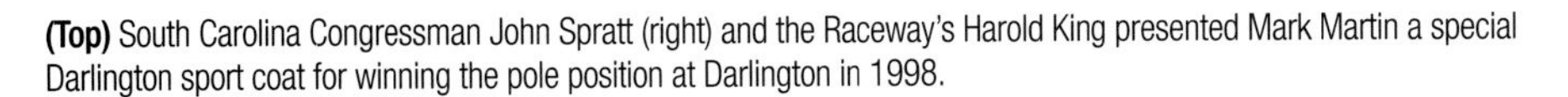

(Top) South Carolina Congressman John Spratt (right) and the Raceway's Harold King presented Mark Martin a special Darlington sport coat for winning the pole position at Darlington in 1998.

(Above) NASCAR's "King" Richard Petty, was inducted into the National Motorsports Press Association Hall of Fame in 1998. Joining him in the celebration were fellow Hall of Famers (l to r, front row) Bobby Allison, Raymond Parks, Jerry Cook, Jack Ingram and Smokey Yunick; (back row) Jack Smith, Benny Parsons, Ralph Moody, Ned Jarrett and Ray fox.

(Right) NASCAR President Bill France, Jr. (center) with Raceway President Red Tyler and driving legend Cale Yarborough, check out construction efforts in the mid-1980s.

(Far Left) Derrike Cope is one of the better golfers among the NASCAR drivers.

(Left) Even Dale Earnhardt shows he knows how to putt.

(Below) Four-time Super Bowl-winning Pittsburgh Steelers quarterback Terry Bradshaw (right) was Grand Marshal for the 1998 TranSouth 400. Here, he converses with NASCAR President Bill France Jr. (left) and TranSouth Financial Corporation President Ken Stephenson.

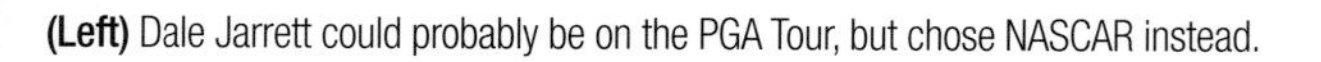

(Left) Dale Jarrett could probably be on the PGA Tour, but chose NASCAR instead.

(Below Left) Jody Ridley gets ready to use the driver.

(Below) Who's the driver in this photo? Jeff Gordon doesn't know if these guys are pointing to him or his club. Joining Gordon is (left to right) Darlington Raceway President Jim Hunter, South Carolina Governor David Beasley, Winston's T. Wayne Robertson and Allen McCall, a member of Darlington's Ambassadors Club.

Past Race Winners/ Miss Southern 500

Diamond Hill Plywood 200
(NASCAR Busch Series, Grand National Division)

1980	David Pearson
1981	Dave Marcis
1982	Geoff Bodine
1983	No Race Held
1984	Ron Bouchard
1985	Jack Ingram
1986	Darrell Waltrip
1987	Dale Earnhardt
1988	Geoff Bodine
1989	Geoff Bodine
1990	Harry Gant
1991	Dale Jarrett
1992	Robert Pressley
1993	Robert Pressley
1994	Mark Martin
1995	Larry Pearson
1996	Mark Martin
1997	Randy LaJoie
1998	Bobby Labonte
1999	Matt Kenseth

Dura Lube 200
(NASCAR Busch Series, Grand National Division)

1983	Neil Bonnett
1984	Ron Bouchard
1985	Darrell Waltrip
1986	Dale Earnhardt
1987	Harry Gant
1988	Harry Gant
1989	Harry Gant
1990	Dale Jarrett
1991	Dale Earnhardt
1992	Michael Waltrip
1993	Mark Martin
1994	Mark Martin
1995	Mark Martin
1996	Terry Labonte
1997	Jeff Burton
1998	Dick Trickle

TranSouth Financial

1957	Fireball Roberts
1958	Curtis Turner
1959	Fireball Roberts
1960	Joe Weatherly
1961	Fred Lorenzen
1962	Nelson Stacy
1963	Joe Weatherly
1964	Fred Lorenzen
1965	Junior Johnson
1966	Richard Petty
1967	Richard Petty
1968	David Pearson
1970	David Pearson
1971	Buddy Baker
1972	David Pearson
1973	David Pearson
1974	David Pearson
1975	Bobby Allison
1976	David Pearson
1977	Darrell Waltrip
1978	Benny Parsons
1979	Darrell Waltrip
1980	David Pearson
1981	Darrell Waltrip
1982	Dale Earnhardt
1983	Harry Gant
1984	Darrell Waltrip
1985	Bill Elliott
1986	Dale Earnhardt
1987	Dale Earnhardt
1988	Lake Speed
1989	Harry Gant
1990	Dale Earnhardt
1991	Ricky Rudd
1992	Bill Elliott
1993	Dale Earnhardt
1994	Dale Earnhardt
1995	Sterling Marlin
1996	Jeff Gordon
1997	Dale Jarrett
1998	Dale Jarrett
1999	Jeff Burton

Pepsi Southern 500

1950	Johnny Mantz
1951	Herb Thomas
1952	Fonty Flock
1953	Buck Baker
1954	Herb Thomas
1955	Herb Thomas
1956	Curtis Turner
1957	Speedy Thompson
1958	Fireball Roberts
1959	Jim Reed
1960	Buck Baker
1961	Nelson Stacy
1962	Larry Frank
1963	Fireball Roberts
1964	Buck Baker
1965	Ned Jarrett
1966	Darel Dieringer
1967	Richard Petty
1968	Cale Yarborough
1969	Lee Roy Yarbrough
1970	Buddy Baker
1971	Bobby Allison
1972	Bobby Allison
1973	Cale Yarborough
1974	Cale Yarborough
1975	Bobby Allison
1976	David Pearson
1977	David Pearson
1978	Cale Yarborough
1979	David Pearson
1980	Terry Labonte
1981	Neil Bonnett
1982	Cale Yarborough
1983	Bobby Allison
1984	Harry Gant
1985	Bill Elliott
1986	Tim Richmond
1987	Dale Earnhardt
1988	Bill Elliott
1989	Dale Earnhardt
1990	Dale Earnhardt
1991	Harry Gant
1992	Darrell Waltrip
1993	Mark Martin
1994	Bill Elliott
1995	Jeff Gordon
1996	Jeff Gordon
1997	Jeff Gordon
1998	Jeff Gordon

Miss Southern 500

Year	Name	Hometown
1953	Martha Dean Chestnut	Conway
1954	Margaret Bryant	Hartsville
1955	Martha Rae Williams	Myrtle Beach
1956	Robin Williamson	Conway
1957	Martha Brannon	Bishopville
1958	Judy Austin	Sumter
1959	Carolyn Melton	Cheraw
1960	Helen Etheridge Hembel	Saluda
1961	Mary Ann Brunnerman	Winnsboro
1962	Joyce Brown	Camden
1963	Nancy Sanders	Chester
1964	Sherry Yvonne Sellers	Darlington
1965	Vicki Johnson	Hartsville
1966	Beth Bryan	Augusta
1967	Roxanne Copeland	Lamar
1968	Vicki Chesser	Mount Pleasant
1969	Susan Gordon	Rock Hill
1970	Nancy Mitchum	Mount Pleasant
1971	Lynn Hollis	Rock Hill
1972	Fran Riggins	Easley
1973	Renee Cousins	Newberry
1974	Cheryl Miles	Johnsonville
1975	Terry Springs	Myrtle Beach
1976	Cindy McDowel	Bishopville
1977	Angela Mixon	Westminster
1978	Lisa Fleming	Anderson
1979	Renee Rodrique	Florence
1980	Karen Huggins	Dillon
1981	Jenny Tedder	Spartanburg
1982	Cathy Knauss	Columbia
1983	Tamalyn Watkins	Charleston
1984	Kim Satterfield	Pelham
1985	Susan Campbell	Camden
1986	Lori Anne Gosnell	Pacolet
1987	Nina Elizabeth Worthy	Summerville
1988	Dawn Michele Dominick	Cayce
1989	Lori Lee Shealy	Lexington
1990	Mary Margaret Roberts	Newberry
1991	Cindy Lee Lewis	Mount Pleasant
1992	Eliza Caughman	Lexington
1993	Cindy Lee Lewis	Mount Pleasant
1994	Amanda Spivey	Spartanburg
1995	Christin Owens	Wagener
1996	Janet Lee Powers	Hartsville
1997	Wendy Crisp	Anderson
1998	Jennifer Broyles	Anderson